DIGITAL
MARKETING
HANDBOOK

5 BOOKS IN 1

- Search Engine Optimization
- Pay Per Click Marketing
- Content Marketing
- Email Marketing
- Social Media Marketing

SHIVANI KARWAL

Digital Marketing Handbook

Publisher: Create Space

First Edition

Table of Contents

Preface

This book was conceived from a need I noticed when I first started out in the digital marketing industry. I felt there was a need for a simple all-inclusive book for beginners covering everything digital. The internet is full of a lot of fluff info on digital marketing and a straightforward and short book that simply explained it all like this one would've saved me an enormous amount of time back then.

My main aim while writing this book was to provide the industry with one single book that left nothing out of the picture and made everything as simple as possible. That's what this book is. **An easy to understand compilation of information about online marketing without any filler content or unnecessary steps. It is short and straight to the point.**

During my time in the industry so far I've come across multiple people who've told me they don't understand online marketing, or it's too complicated and I don't blame them. Online marketing is explained through this filter that makes it all seem so complicated. Well I'm here to change that.

If you enjoy reading this book, feel free to share your thoughts and rate on Amazon and Goodreads. You can get in touch with me at: **shivani@digiologist.com** and send requests and feedback to **feedback@digiologist.com**. You can also join the Digiologist Facebook group, which is a community of other students who have also read the book and taken the course: **www.facebook.com/**

If you want to take your learning to the next level, check out the **Digital Marketing Course at www.digiologist.com.**

I hope that after reading this book, you are able to experience the power of online marketing and it brings your business massive success.

Thank you for reading!

Shivani Karwal

Part 1: Getting Started

Getting Started

Let's start off by going into what marketing was like before. Traditional mediums of marketing such as print ads, billboards, radio ads etc have been around since commerce existed around the early 1900s. Basically, ever since there has been something to sell, marketing has existed. For most of the time since existence, marketing has been offline and through mediums such as posters, billboards, print ads in newspapers or magazines, radio etc.

These mediums still prevail, but come the late 1990s, the internet came into existence and online became a whole new medium to market through. SEO, PPC, Content Marketing were all in the early phases of development at that time. Social media came into play a bit later in the early 2000s. Presently, various elements of digital marketing are in full play and it is more important than ever for your business to have a strong presence online. Considering the scope of the Internet, being found is now more important than ever. The Internet is accessible to almost anyone and you need to take advantage of that.

Thus it is very important to not only concentrate on traditional methods such as print ads, radio etc., but to explore the online world for your marketing efforts. There are over 3 billion Internet users worldwide and more than 70% of them use it daily! If your business is not online, think of all the possible customers you're losing out on and all the money you're not making!

Your business could make 10, 20, 30... who knows how many times more money with a digital presence.

What is Online Marketing?

Online marketing, also called digital marketing or internet marketing, is simply marketing through the internet. It involves using the web to promote a product or service. It mainly uses electronic devices such as PCs, laptops, phones and tablets to promote the message through online connectivity. All this can be done through many ways such as search engine optimization, pay per click marketing, content marketing, social media marketing, email marketing. These methods have been discussed in detail later on in the book.

For setting everything up, the first thing you need to do is choose a domain name for your website. Some business owners underestimate the importance of having a website and skip making one which is a bad move. They say a business without a website is like a man without a face. A faceless man cannot tell you anything about him. Similarly, a business without a website cannot give out important information like what the business is, information about the products/services, location, phone number etc. Sure you can put all of that on your social media, but it is no replacement for a proper website. If you do not have a site, your are suffering and losing possible business. Did you know more than 3.5 billion searches are conducted on Google each day?

Everything is moving online now and so you need to have a strong digital presence. A large number of searches are conducted online and a part of them are for your industry. If you do not have a website, you simply have no chance of ranking for those search queries and have possible customers find you.

Choosing a good domain name is important. A domain name is what the visitor types in the address bar to reach your site, sort of like an electronic address. It's what your audience remembers you by so it needs to be relevant and memorable.

As a business owner, the best domain name option would be to go with your brand name for relevancy and brand positioning purposes. But the domain names we want are not always available. In case you've been put into that situation or simply want a domain different from your brand name, start by brainstorming ideas. A good domain name that is still available can take a bit of time to find.

Characteristics of a Good Domain Name:

1. Relevancy: Try using your domain name as a branding tool. If you can use your company name as your domain, it'll help a lot in brand positioning. Branded domains help in the long run as they help create credibility while promoting yourself.
2. Length: The shorter, the better. Long domains are just a nuisance to remember and type. Aim

for 10-15 characters.

3. Easy to Remember: A catchy and easy to remember domain is what you should aim for so people don't have trouble finding it when they need to.
4. Easy to Spell and Pronounce: The domain name being easy to spell and pronounce is important too. You don't want people misspelling your link and not being able to reach your site.
5. Without Hyphens: Hyphens take away from the brand image, have no SEO value and look spammy, so avoid them.

A domain name does not need to be an exact match to the keyword you're trying to rank for. Although it helps to an extent, it is not mandatory and ends up looking unprofessional. Most sites that rank are branded non-keyword names anyway.

Also keep in mind the parts of a site structure and the options you have for them:

1. TLD: The top level domain is the part of the site address that comes after the dot. Some examples of TLD options available are: .com, .net, .org, .gov, .edu, .co, .info etc.
2. SLD: The second level domain is the domain name itself and the part of the site address located to the left of the dot. It is the part of the domain name you choose i.e. the name you register.

3. Subdomain: The subdomain, which is also the third level domain, is the part before the SLD.
4. Subdirectory: The subdirectory is the part after the slash after .com.

Here are a few examples to make it clearer:

Eg 1: www.digiologist.com

TLD: .com
SLD: digiologist
Subdomain: n/a
Subdirectory: n/a

Eg 2: www.digiologist.com/blog

TLD: .com
SLD: digiologist
Subdomain: n/a
Subdirectory: blog

Eg 3: www.blog.digiologist.com

TLD: .com
SLD: digiologist
Subdomain: blog
Subdirectory: n/a

First choose your domain name according to your business name. Then choose the TLD according to your industry and location. Most people go with .com but if you're targeting a specific geographical area only, feel free to go with the one for your country. Also keep in mind the other options:

Examples of Different TLDs and Who Uses Them:

.com: Stands for 'commercial' and can be used by anyone in general
.org: Used by non-profit organizations
.net: Used by anyone but used to be for the main 'umbrella' site of a group of smaller sites
.co: Stands for 'company'
.info: For informational sites
.edu: For educational sites
.gov: For government sites
.biz: For business sites
.int: For international organizations

Once you have made your choice, head over to a domain registrar and register it. A registrar I've been using for many years now is Hostgator. Some other popular ones are GoDaddy and Bluehost. There are many other options out there so feel free to look around. Domain names are pretty affordable and usually cost around $10 to $15 per year. You'll also need hosting for your site as well, which you can get from the same registrar.

After buying your domain name and getting hosting, you'll need to set everything up like Whois info, domain email etc in your account. One of the things you may need to set up and choose between is either a subdomain or subdirectory, if you require them. You'll need this for setting up the blog section of your site. More on the benefits of business blogging is in the content marketing section.

Subdomain vs. Subdirectory:

Subdomains and subdirectories are used for creating specific areas on your site for particular content. They're great for sectioning off parts of your site topic wise. You can easily create and delete subdomains and subdirectories in your cPanel so look into your registrar specific instructions for that. But which of the two is better?

Subdirectories are the more popular choice and what I use on my site personally. Google considers a subdomain as a separate domain. So if you're using a subdomain, you're basically diluting your sites value between your domain and subdomain(s). A subdirectory on the other hand is considered a part of your domain and a much better choice as it's able to take the advantage of your main domains already built up authority.

Choosing the Right TLD:

Making the right choice when selecting a TLD is important. If you're doubtful about your businesses future plans, and don't know if you'll be expanding to other countries and even niches, it's a good idea to stick to the popular and safe .com option. If you're sure about your business niche and want to be able to tell what your site is about in an instant and appear unique in search results, you can go for a relevant gTLD (generic TLD) that is very specific to your industry such as .accountant, .doctor etc.

However, the thing about all these new TLDs though, is that their use is not very popular right now and it is expected that their growth is going to be slow and gradual. They also don't appear trustworthy to most people as they're not familiar with them. My preference, and what I use for my own sites is the common .com TLD. Going with a more common TLD like .com or other ones if relevant like .co, .net, .org etc or a country specific one if you plan on sticking there is presently a better choice. But if your company is not international and you have no plans of taking it international, a ccTLD (country specific TLD) is the way to go. A country specific TLD helps in ranking higher in local search results and the local versions of search engines, which are geo targeted by default. If you have multiple locations, you can even fit the ccTLD into your subdomain or as a subdirectory like: ca.digiologist.com or digiologist.com/ca.

Do TLDs Affect Rankings?

Any TLD can rank in search engines whether it's an old and commonly used TLD or a new one, as long as the TLD you've chosen is relevant and applicable. The reason why we don't really see many uncommon TLDs rank such as .lawyer or .travel etc, is because not many people are using them. Because they're not used as widely as .com, people tend to believe they are harder to rank but that is not true. But at the same time, they don't have any added advantages either. They're only good for relevancy. As far as rankings go, any TLD you choose will be fine, as long as it is relevant. But as far as looks and credibility goes, as discussed above, uncommon gTLDs do tend to appear untrustworthy as they are unknown and haven't made their mark yet. So if possible, stick to getting a .com.

Where to Start?

The first thing you need ofcourse is a website. Along with getting a domain name, here are some things you'll need:

1. Domain Name
2. Hosting
3. Content Management System
4. Site Design or Template
5. Domain Name Email

Once you have all that, you'll need to create an effective site map, optimize your site and set up analytics. All this has been discussed in upcoming chapters. But for now, let's talk about the basics on how to get everything set up.

Once you've registered your domain and have hosting, you need to choose a CMS i.e. content management system and you have a variety of options for that, some of which are Wordpress, Drupal, Joomla etc.

A content management system is like a web application for presenting, creating and controlling your HTML content. Basically, a CMS helps you bring your information available to your audiences in an easy and polished manner and as the name suggests, it simply helps you *manage your content*.

The three CMS's above are just the most popular ones I've mentioned but there are many more options out there. However, it's a good idea to stick to a popular one as there are more choices for plugins and templates for them and also more tutorials and support.

The most popular CMS is Wordpress and what I personally use. It's an excellent platform that is so easy to use thanks to the numerous tutorials out there. It's simple to set up and has some really great plugins and templates developed for it.

To make your choice on which CMS to use, search up on the CMS options out there and the pros and cons of each. Most probably Wordpress is your best bet but in the odd case you need more features, read up on other systems.

Website Design - DIY or Hire Someone?

You have two options for your site design and development - either do it yourself or hire someone to do it for you. This decision really depends on what you're going for. Do you have a very specific picture in mind of how your site should be? If so, hiring a designer is the correct route. On the other hand, if you're okay with using a readymade template and tweaking it a bit, just do it yourself. There are many really great themes out there you can use.

One great way to find a good theme to use is by checking out a variety of sites and inserting them into www.whatwpthemeisthat.com. That only works for sites using a theme and Wordpress of course, but it helpful in choosing themes for sites. By doing so, you can see a live use of a number of themes and see them in action.

For making the right choice, another factor to consider is the safety of the theme. Read up reviews on it to make sure it is legitimate and doesn't contain spammy code at the backend that will land you in trouble later on. A great tip is to always go for premium paid themes to avoid that. They're quite affordable and are usually priced around a one time fee of $60 to $80 on an average. Read up reviews on popular themes for specific uses.

There are themes that are excellent for blogging, but they won't be suitable for a business and then there are themes that are great for businesses but they may not be suitable for an ecommerce business where you need to set up shopping carts, checkout pages and payment gateways. So choose according to your needs, looks of the theme and legitimacy.

It's also a good idea to choose a theme that looks near to what you have in mind for your site so you only have to customize a little bit. A point to note here is that you can't customize a theme to completely change its look. You can mostly only really tweak sizes, fonts, spaces, colours etc. For a fully customized site that matches exactly what you have in mind, it's a better idea to hire someone. I have personally always used premium themes and tweaked them according to my liking instead of hiring someone. You'll be surprised at the professional look of some of the themes out there.

Choosing a template vs. hiring a developer also depends on the size your site is going to be. Here's an example: If you have a small clothing shop around the corner and want a site for it, you're better off using a template and building it yourself. But if you're starting your own clothing line on the scales of let's Tommy Hilfiger, you definitely need a developer - a theme just won't do.

At the end of the day it all really comes down to resources. Website design can cost around $3,000 plus. Of course some companies charge way more than that, but in that approximate amount, you can get a pretty awesome design done. If you have that amount to spare and require a custom design, go for having someone else do it for you. On the other hand if you want to cut back on costs in the beginning, then getting a theme is a better choice.

Types of Site Design: Page Layouts

The types of website layouts are important and matter because they change based on the device the site is being viewed in. Since a large chunk of people use mobiles and tablets to surf the internet, you need to make sure your site looks good on cell phones and tablets. If you're using a theme, make sure it is responsive. If you're having someone design for you, tell them what you need.

Below are some different types of page layouts:

1. Fixed: Also known as 'static' pages, they do not change based on browser size and device. This is the least preferred layout as it looks fuzzy on larger devices and makes everything hard to read on smaller devices. Have you ever tried surfing a site on your phone where the text is too hard to read and you have to zoom in? Those are static pages and they are not mobile friendly.
2. Liquid: Also known as 'fluid' layouts, they allow the page content to fill the width of the screen no matter what size it is. This doesn't work well with larger devices. In such cases, what would

normally be an entire paragraph can end up being stretched and turning into only a few lines.

3. **Responsive:** Responsive layouts change as the browser increases or decreases in size. They are the best layouts to go with due to their adaptability and are mobile friendly.

Different Methods of Digital Marketing:

There are numerous ways to market your business online. Each of these mediums requires different skill sets and each have their pros and cons. Some business owners go for one of them and choose to master it, while others go for many or all. I use every single one of them. You too can choose to do all of them and become really good at them too. Just read this book and apply what you learn.

Main Methods of Digital Marketing:

1. Search Engine Optimization
2. Pay Per Click Advertising
3. Email Marketing
4. Social Media Marketing
5. Content Marketing

I've discussed the above methods briefly below but for the in-depth how-to part, refer to the associated sections for each.

Search Engine Optimization:

Search Engine Optimization, commonly referred to as SEO is the process of getting a site to rank in search engines such as Google and improving the ranks with time till you rank well. SEO is free, which means it is not advertising. It can cost you if you hire an agency to do it for you of course, but if you do it yourself, the only resource you're spending is your time. With SEO you're mainly applying strategies to make your site more visible in search engines i.e. make it appear in search results as high as possible.

The ideal rank you want your site to get is on the first page of the search engine in the first 5 results at least, but aiming for the top 3 with ranking at the first position being your ultimate goal. Did you know that most searchers look at the first 3 search results only? Out of all of the traffic a particular keyword gets for search results, approximately 40% users click on the page ranking at the first position and over 90% people do not scroll past the first page of the results. So not only is it important to atleast get your pages in the search results, but it is even more important to get them to rank towards the top.

Search engine optimization is a powerful strategy for marketing your business online. The section of this book on SEO will break everything down for you and make it all easy. SEO is the type of online marketing that requires the most all round ability ranging from technical and analytical skills to creativity. While activities such as social media and email marketing are great and helpful, it is SEO that usually brings in the most amount of traffic.

Pay Per Click and Display Advertising:

Pay per click marketing, popularly referred to as PPC, is the method of online marketing that shows results the fastest. It is however, also the costliest one. PPC basically involves making an ad for your site and having it show up as a search result in the paid section of the results page at the top and in the sidebar. PPC allows you to instantly show up in search results (in the paid section) unlike SEO, which can take months of effort at times for you to even rank. Since you're paying for PPC, it needs to be done with lots of care. If it's not done properly, it can end up costing you tons of wasted money.

When we hear PPC we immediately think of opening an account, writing the ad copy and hitting go and watching visitors and leads pour in. However it is so much more than that. Careful keyword research and selection needs to be done before the ad copy is even made. More on this is discussed in the PPC section.

Email Marketing:

Email marketing, as the name suggests, involves sending promotional messages using email as the medium. This is permission based, meaning you make an email list based on who opts in and send them commercial emails. You can send emails to a purchased list as well instead of building one but we'll discuss later on why that's a bad idea. If you are able to build a strong list of subscribers, they act as a loyal fan base and audience that is always at your disposal to send off information to instantly. This is great for new product launch announcements.

Content Marketing:

Content marketing is actually the easiest to do to stand out, because most businesses, sadly, are not doing it right. Most are doing content marketing simply to create content that can rank and they fail to create value for the person reading. They're creating content just for the sake of putting content out there. It's a simple formula - create engaging, valuable and well-written content, and leads will come rushing towards you. When you work hard in creating amazing content that provides value, there is absolutely no way it won't be successful. People read your content, like it and are then more interested in what else you have to offer. Everything that provides value is always well accepted. Content marketing helps send out your message without any cost. The place where you share this content is on your sites blog and social media. I write this assuming you have a lot of knowledge about your niche since you have a business in it. Since you already have the knowledge, you don't need to spend hours researching what to write about. All you need to do is write it and share it with the world. When others see you as being knowledgeable about your niche and producing thought leadership content, they can trust you a lot better and think, this person seems to know what they're talking about, and they automatically come to you as leads. Make your content so good that they want to buy from you without a thought.

Simply writing filler content for ranking purposes is a complete waste of time and what I see most businesses doing. You don't need to produce content very frequently. Concentrate more on the quality rather than quantity. I personally do not post on Digiologist every day because all I care about is quality. I'd rather do one to two posts and videos a week or biweekly and make it amazing than to post mediocre content daily. You have to stand out somehow. Make your posts memorable and talk worthy so they're shared and spread across more people.

Social Media Marketing:

Social media marketing involves getting your message across by sharing and interacting on social networks across the web i.e. social media sites, some well known examples of which are platforms like Facebook, Twitter, Instagram and Pinterest to name a few. Social media has explosively grown over the past decade. If done right, it can do wonders for you and help you grow so large that you'd never imagined was even possible.

Your customers are online and interacting on sites like Facebook and Twitter on a daily basis. They are already there and all you need to do now is find them and establish contact and build a relationship. Since your customers are actively a part of social media, there is absolutely no excuse for your business not be a part of it.

Above were just some of the main methods of marketing your business online. The individual sections of this book cover each strategy more detail.

Helpful Sites and Set Up Plugins:

Domain Registrars and Hosting Providers:

Hostgator: www.hostgator.com
GoDaddy: www.godaddy.com
BlueHost: www.bluehost.com

Sites:

Official Wordpress forum to discuss the platform: en.forums.wordpress.com
Wordpress support: en-ca.wordpress.org/support
To find out which Wordpress theme is in use: whatwpthemeisthat.com
Design Inspiration: Awwwards (awwwards.com) has screenshots of some of the best web design out there.

Plugins:

Wordpress Cache: Speeds up your site. There are various versions to choose form such as W3 Total Cache and W3 Super Cache based on your needs.
BackWPup: Creates automatic backups of your wordpress site content. Get it at www.wordpress.org/plugins/backwpup
WordFence Security: Ensures Wordpress security to prevent break ins. Get it at wordpress.org/plugins/wordfence
SEO by Yoast: Great SEO plugin for Wordpress that handles on-page SEO flawlessly. Get it, along with

other Yoast plugins at yoast.com/wordpress/plugins
Redirection: Helps easily manage 301 redirects and 404 errors. Get it at wordpress.org/plugins/redirection

*All of the sites and plugins above are for Wordpress as it is a more popular choice than other content management systems.

Digital Marketing FAQs:

How is digital marketing different from traditional marketing and do I need it?

Traditional marketing mediums such as print, television, radio etc are slowly losing their audience reach to digital marketing due to the advancement of the web and the massive amount of people using the internet on a regular basis. Digital marketing allows you to get your brand in front of those masses with many benefits such as reduced cost, demographic and geographic targeting, measurable results through detailed analytics etc. The internet is where people are spending their time and your business needs to have a strong digital presence to take advantage of that.

Do I need online marketing even if I don't sell my products/services online?

Yes. Even if you don't sell your products or services online, you should still market your business online. Having an optimized website and social media presence will inform more people about your business. So even if your sales will end up taking place offline, it's good to build a presence online to create awareness and generate leads.

Do I need a website?

Your business website can serve a variety of

purposes such as being your online portfolio, your space to give information about your products/services and contact info and opportunity to build your brand. Having a business website is a means to keep your customers informed. Most importantly, it helps you in getting found by ranking in search engines. You can't rank if you don't have a website.

Should I do it all myself or hire someone?

Whether you can do it yourself or not mainly depends on your learning curve and how much time and resources you have. The amount of time it will take depends on if you're just starting out or have a bit of a strategy going on and also how strong your competitors online profiles are. My suggestion to you would be to read this book, watch the video course on the Digiologist website, implement everything and give your efforts some time to start showing results. Hiring someone to do it will cost you so it all comes down to resources.

How much does it cost?

If you're doing it all on your own, the only thing you'll be paying for is pay per click ad spend, which is just one of the ways of marketing your business online. Everything else from SEO to social media, email marketing, content marketing etc doesn't have any costs, except for any softwares or tools you may need. Digital marketing will cost you if you decide to hire someone to do it for you and the quotes for that vary from company to company and are also based on your needs so there is no definite figure but on an average be prepared to shell out a couple grand monthly for a decent agency.

How much time do I need to put in it?

If you're just starting out, the effort you need to put in will be more. You'll have to set up your website and all your social profiles from start, then optimize them, set up email newsletters, make a content schedule etc. The initial efforts for setting up take up the most time and after that it's mostly just upkeep and improvement to be done based on results. Sometimes complications can also arise like penalties, which will take additional time. Time wise, the number can go from a few hours a day for small to medium sized business to even all your time for larger companies. Ranking wise, it can take less than a month to rank for less competitive keywords and many months for competitive ones. You should start implementing your strategy and measure results to get an idea of the timeline as it is based on many factors like your industry, how strong your competitors are, how established you are, how much time and effort you can put in.

Part 2: Search Engine Optimization

Introduction to Search Engine Optimization

Search engine optimization involves improving the rank of website in search engine results organically through non-paid strategies with the aim of having the site rank as high as possible. A search engine is a site that searches for results from the web pertaining to the keywords or keyphrases inputted by a user. In simple words, whatever you input into a search engine, it gives you results from the web it thinks are about your keyword and most relevant. Some other search engines besides Google are Yahoo and Bing.

How do search engines work? Search engines are able to bring back results through crawling, indexing and retrieving.

During crawling, robots a.k.a spiders scan the information and data on websites such as the page titles, image tags, headings, content, keywords used and more. Since crawlers do this, it is automated and done insanely fast. Indexing involves compiling all of the data discovered during the crawling process. Retrieving, involves getting the user a list of the most accurate results from the site pages crawled in relation to the search query inputted.

Let's demonstrate the power of search engines with the help of an example. Open Google and type in the term 'car dealer'. The .com version of Google brings back 170 millions results! Yet Google was still able to rank all 170 million of those sites and even chose one of them to rank #1. How did it decide all that?

Google has a long list of ranking factors, some of which are:

1. Keywords used
2. Image optimization
3. Inbound and outbound links
4. Domain age and authority
5. Social shares
6. Site speed

The above are just some of the main ones. There are over 100 such ranking factors, a complete list of which can be found online. But keep in mind that the lists of ranking factors online are ones compiled by the industry and not Google itself. Google has never released a list of its ranking factors and states that its reason for doing so is its frequent changes in its ranking algorithm.

SEO efforts can mainly be categorized into three parts:

1. On-page SEO
2. Off-page SEO
3. Local SEO

For a brief differentiation between the three, on-page SEO deals with everything you do on your business site, off-page SEO deals with what is done on external sites and local SEO includes both on-site and off-site (but mostly off-site) efforts done to increase rankings in local search results.

On-page SEO:

On-page SEO involves making efforts on the actual site itself using relevant keywords on your site and having a good site structure. This mostly involves two things: using relevant keywords wherever necessary throughout the site content and having a clean site structure. Some of the on-page elements that need to be optimized are the title tags, meta descriptions, headers, page content, image alt text. This is done by placing keywords you want to rank for in the content across these elements. On-page SEO also involves having a good site structure that is clean and easy for the search engine crawlers to read and index. Because on-page takes place on your site, it is all in your control and that makes it easy. And since it is so easy, most sites have their on-page SEO going strong, so that also makes it less impactful on rankings. That doesn't mean that it's not important. It just means that mostly everyone has their on-page SEO right so only relying on on-page techniques won't help you stand out in front of search engines.

Off-page SEO:

Off-page SEO is more difficult and what takes more time and effort for businesses to get right. Off-page, as the name suggests, takes place on external sites and the external parties make the decisions. Off-page SEO mainly involves two things: building incoming links from external sites pointing to your site and getting social shares of your site content. Even though social shares are a large part of social media, social signals such as your content being socially shared are valuable to search engines and a part of off-page optimization. Off-page SEO gives search engines an indication of how your site is doing compared to others. Each link pointing to your site and social share of your site content is like a vote of approval from others. And the more of them you get, the better you appear for search engines. Of course a variety of factors matter like the quality and relevancy of the sites linking to you, which have been discussed later on.

Local SEO:

Local SEO is very important for businesses with a physical address or those specifically targeting a particular geographical region. If your business has a physical location, local SEO can help you rank in search results for searches being conducted near your location and make you visible to searchers in your area, thus placing you in front of possible customers location wise. You must have come across local search results before while searching for a product or service and having the results come up with a map or list showing local businesses providing that product or service that are practicing in your location. When you get search results that are located near you, it is because of local SEO.

Steps Involved: On-page SEO

On-page SEO mainly deals with strategies that take place on the parts of your site, so it has nothing to do with external sites.

On-page SEO efforts involve two things:

1. Optimizing: Optimizing the page content, headings, title tags, meta descriptions etc. is done by inserting keywords in them and the keywords used are the ones you want to rank for when people search for them. These keywords are selected based on their traffic and competitiveness level, a process that is known as keyword research.
2. Having a site structure that is clean and easy to navigate

Site Structure:

Getting your site structure correct is very important. The way your site is laid out and content is organized, stored and presented affects not only your sites user friendly ability, but also the ability of search engines to be able to find and crawl your site. A clean and well laid out site structure is easier for search engines to find and read and improves your crawl rate, thus increasing your chances of ranking.

Your site structure is the foundation of your site and the first and most important step. If this step is done wrong, no matter what you do after and how amazing your content is, it won't be of any use if the site structure is weak. A good site structure is the very core of good SEO.

Make sure your site is not invisible to search engines. A site can become invisible to search engines if the site structure is not readable by site crawlers. How can you remove this problem or have it not occur?

- Create more links on your site by interlinking your pages.
- Create a sitemap and upload to Google webmasters.
- Create a sitemap for your readers that is on your actual site. This one refers to the one created for users, which is different from the one you create for Google Webmasters.

How can you find out if your site is being crawled and indexed by search engines? Try testing it with Google.

Open google.com and type in:

site:domain.com

Enter this without http or www.

So for example, for the Digiologist site, I'd type in:

site:digiologist.com

If you search the above in Google, it tells you how many results it found. Currently as I'm writing this, the above search results in '2 results' as the site only really has the home page and an about page and hasn't officially launched yet. What's important is that Google comes back with results for the above search query and it should be doing the same for your site.

Some things to consider while deciding your site structure:

1. Deciding your menu (navigation) structure
2. Number of drop downs in the navigation
3. Permalink structures
4. The internal linking structure

How to Have a Good Site Structure:

1. Have a structure that is well laid out and easy for your visitors to navigate through.
2. Have a home-page button on all pages that your visitors can click on when they reach the deeper pages of your site.
3. Don't over complicate your navigation bar hierarchy. Too many drop downs will confuse the user.
4. Create a descriptive URL structure that explains your structure and that all your permalinks will follow. For e.g., if your business

has multiple locations, set the URL structures to look like example.com/locations/toronto instead of example.com/toronto.

5. Create your site navigation and content in HTML or CSS instead of JavaScript.
6. Develop an internal linking structure.
7. Instead of deleting pages and creating 404s, redirect them through 301s.

How to Create a Sitemap

Once you've decided your layout and your site is up and running, create an XML sitemap and upload it to your Google Webmasters account. This sitemap is like a map or layout for your site and shows all of the pages and the hierarchy of their organization. It makes it a lot easier for search engines to crawl your website.

Generating an xml sitemap for your site is easy. Just follow the instructions on sitemap generators like xml-sitemaps.com, download the file when done and upload to your sites Google Webmaster Tools account. You can do that by clicking 'sitemaps' in the left hand sidebar, click 'add a sitemap' and upload the file. If you do not have a Google Webmasters Tools account yet, get one by signing up at google.com/webmasters. Having a GWT account helps in keeping you up to date on any problems occurring on your site.

How to Create a Robots.txt File:

A robots.txt file instructs search engine robots how to crawl the site and which pages to skip crawling on a website and not include in search results. These are pages you don't want to be shown in search results.

Some examples of cases where a robots.txt files can be used:

1. To block images from being crawled in the case of the site owner not wanting them to rank in search engines.
2. To tell search engines to ignore duplicate content on your site.
3. To prevent search engines from accessing certain areas of your site you don't want to rank such as old outdated content.
4. To tell search engines to ignore outdated content on your site.
5. To prevent your entire website from being crawled and shown in results.

If you think you or someone else may have created a robots.txt file for your site and want to see how it is set up, check it out at www.yoursite.com/robots.txt with your site domain.

To make a robots.txt file, follow the following format:

User-agent: *
Disallow: /example/

In place of example, type in the page you don't want to be crawled. For example, if you want your images and admin area pages to be blocked from crawlers, your file would contain the following:

User-agent: *
Disallow: /images/
Disallow: /wp-admin/

Note the above is just an example and will only work if the above matches your actual pages. So if you want to block your images and they are located at yoursite.com/library/images/, the above needs to be changed to: Disallow: /library/images/. You mainly need to put in the part of URL of the pages after .com between the two slashes.

Create the above file as a word document, save and upload to the root directory of your website.

This file needs to be created with extreme care. Even a slight mistake can end up excluding all or many of your pages from being indexed and preventing you from ranking in search engines, resulting in lost traffic and leads. If you don't have any pages to block from search engines, skip creating a robots.txt file because you don't need it.

Dealing With Not Found Pages and Redirects: 404s, 301s and 302s:

Not found error pages will occur if you remove a lot of pages and don't redirect those pages to elsewhere. For example, let's suppose you have a lot of blog posts on your company blog from the past and some of the content is outdated and you no longer want to update it and remove the pages without redirecting them after removing the content. The pages will then no longer have the content but the URLs of those pages which once existed, will have links pointing to them from other sites. You will have people clicking on those links, only to end up opening a 'not found' error page on your site. These not found pages are also called 404 pages because of their HTTP status code.

The three popular codes you need to know are:

404: A missing page that has been deleted
301: A permanent redirect
302: A temporary redirect

A 404 page error usually shows up whe1n an old pages content is deleted or moved without redirecting the old pages URL. If the content is moved, the old link should be redirected to the new one where the new content is. If the content is deleted, the old link should be redirected to the home page (or a page most relevant to the old content). 404 error pages also come up when a link is misspelled or a link is entered that never existed.

For the cases where the content of a page has permanently moved to another page or you just want a page to permanently redirect to another page with similar content, use a 301 redirect, which is a permanent redirect. A 302 redirect, which is a temporary redirect can be used if the page you want to redirect to is under construction or if you want all clicks to a page under temporary construction to point to another page instead while it is being built.

Do 404s hurt your site? 404s are something all sites have from time to time so don't fret over them. But having too many 404 error pages will lead to more bounces and more visitors turning away from your site if they can't find what they're looking for and all they're getting are error pages.

A good practice is to create a custom 404 page so in case of unwanted and unavoidable error pages coming up for visitors when they misspell links or enter in pages that don't exist, they are presented with a custom 404 page giving them options to check out other pages like the home page, about page, service page etc.

To create a custom 404 page just install a custom 404 page plugin for Wordpress like 'Custom 404 Pro' (wordpress.org/plugins/custom-404-pro) for your CMS and follow the instructions it comes with. You can also manually do this from your cPanel but that is a more complicated process.

To implement 301 or 302 redirects, use the 'Redirection' plugin for Wordpress at wordpress.org/plugins/redirection. Again, you can manually do this from your cPanel by editing your ht.access file but that process is a lot more complicated and the above plugin gets the same results.

Conducting Keyword Research:

Keyword research is the first and most important step of optimization. All your optimization efforts should be based on the keywords you choose. Optimizing without keywords is like strategizing without goals. The keywords you choose are the ones you aim to rank for. They need to be chosen with care and research and numbers to back your decision.

Keyword research doesn't involve just choosing a bunch of keywords relevant to you and stuffing your site pages with them. Yes relevance is important, but numbers are important too. You need to look into how much traffic those keywords are getting and how tough it is to rank for them. There are keywords that are highly relevant but also very competitive to rank for so going after them may not always be the best decision. It's better to spend your time and effort on keywords that are less competitive.

Some things you should ask yourself while choosing

your keywords:

1. Are the keywords you're choosing being searched enough times for you to get decent traffic from them if you rank?
2. Are the keywords you're choosing easy to rank for or will they take months or maybe even a years worth of effort to show up for?
3. Do the keywords have enough traffic from locations your product or service is sold in?
4. Are the keywords relevant to your business?

How do you find out all of the above? Sign into the AdWords Google Keyword Planner tool located at adwords.google.ca/KeywordPlanner. It will give you all of the information about your keywords of choice such as their competitiveness level and search volume.

Here's an outline of the steps to take while conducting keyword research:

Brainstorm a list of all possible keywords and keyphrases you can think of. You can do this a few ways. Make an entire list of keywords that are relevant to your business that people might be putting into search engines to find businesses like yours. Stretch those keywords into keyphrases and make a list of those too. Come up with different ways of saying the same thing (use synonyms) and expand your list.

For example, if you have a luxury jewellery store, just some of the examples of keywords that immediately come to mind are:

- gold jewellery
- platinum jewellery
- silver jewellery
- diamond jewellery

These are just the main basic keywords. Add more detail and you get:

- gold jewellery store
- platinum jewellery store
- silver jewellery store
- diamond jewellery store

Add even more detail and you get keyphrases like 'buy gold jewellery online' and so on for platinum, silver etc. You can also add location modifiers for wherever your store is located and get 'gold jewellery store Toronto' and so on. You can also create a second version of all of your keyphrases with 'jewelry' instead of 'jewellery'. They're just two different ways of spelling the word in different countries. Look into such modifiers. You can also go longtail and make them in the form of questions like: where to buy gold jewellery. You can also add queries for additional services you offer or things you think people might be looking for such as 'where to get jewellery repaired', 'ring cleaning' etc.

My biggest tip is to put yourself in the shoes of the customer and think from their perspective. In this case, you'd think to yourself, if you were a customer and were looking for a jewellery store in Toronto, what are all the possible search queries you could input into a search engine to find what you're looking for.

If you've exhausted your ideas, you can take the help of the keyword idea tools out there like Ubersuggest (ubersuggest.org). And here's a bonus tip: use Google suggest. Google suggest is the list of suggestions that appear at the bottom of the search results page and are based off of what people are already searching.
Then add all of the keywords into the Google Keyword Planner located at adwords.google.ca/KeywordPlanner.

The Adwords keyword planner is meant for choosing keywords for your pay per click campaign but it gives the same information you need for choosing keywords for your on-page optimization as well. Enter your search phrases into the tool and it will come back with metrics such as search volume, keyword ideas and competition to rank.

You mainly want to find the golden opportunities here i.e. keywords that have the combination of high search volume and low to medium ranking competition. These keywords are the ones that will be easier to rank and have enough search traffic so they're worth putting the effort into. It'll be easier to do this in an excel sheet so import your results and sort your sheet. A thing to note here is that the keyword competition score in the tool is actually for paid rankings so a good idea is to get a more accurate score from a keyword difficulty tool for organic search results. Though it is generally similar in most cases because a keyword that is tough for pay per click is usually tough to rank for organically as well too, so start off by using the Adwords Keyword Planner.

After entering all of your brainstormed keywords into the tool and choosing the ones with the best combinations of high search traffic and low to medium competition, download the chosen ones in excel format. Out of your final chosen keyword, based on the numbers, choose your primary and secondary keywords. Your primary keyword is the main keyword you want to rank for and the one you think will get you the most business if you rank for it. The primary keyword is the one you will use in the content on your main pages like the home page and other important pages like the about page, service page etc. These pages are the ones with the most power and so your primary keywords should be used in their content. Your secondary keywords will be used in the content on less powerful pages like blog content pages. Once you've matched your keywords with preferred pages based on their importance, you're ready to start optimizing.

Optimizing Your Site Content:

Once you've decided which pages you want to rank for specific keywords i.e. which keywords you want to use on specific pages, add the keywords into the content of that page across the following on-page elements:

- Title tag*
- Meta description tag
- Meta tags (only useful for search engines like Yahoo, Bing. Not Google)
- Article title/Page Title*
- Content Headings
- In the material of the content
- URL of the page
- Description and Alt text of the images
- Article tags

*Note that the page/article title and title tag are both different. They are both titles for the page but the title tag is shown as the title in search results and the page/article title is shown as the title on your site. You can keep them both the same or slightly change them as well.

To add the keywords to the title tag, meta tags, meta description, get a good SEO plugin for your CMS. A good one for Wordpress is the Yoast SEO plugin, which is available at: wordpress.org/plugins/wordpress-seo. After installing the plugin, you'll get space for adding your tags and descriptions for each page.

The title tag will appear at the top of your listing in the search engine results as the heading and the meta description will appear under it. This is what people see when they see your website ranking in search results and decide whether to click on your site or not, so they need to be unique, informative, useful and captivating enough to get the maximum clicks.

In addition to the above, it is important to keep in mind the keyword density of the content and to try to place the keywords in the beginning in the first 100 words atleast. The keyword density is the percentage of the number of times the keyword appears in the body of the content based on the total number of words of the content. Try keeping the density between 2% to 3% and try to make this look as natural as possible so don't repeat your keyword too many times. It is important to write the content for your reader first and foremost and secondly for search engine ranking purposes. If you simply add your keyword way too many times in your content for ranking purposes, your content is going to end up not being very useful to the reader and they will shut your page immediately, thus spending less time on your site, which Google takes as your page not being useful and lowers your rankings. So keyword stuffing will backfire on you. Also put in effort into improving your page load times, which again, is a search engine ranking factor.

The page title, meta tags and meta description, optimizing is done using the SEO plugin and the rest is taken care through your CMS itself. You can use your keywords in image descriptions, alt text, page content etc. while writing it in your CMS like you normally do.

Steps Involved: Off-Page SEO

Off-page SEO, as the name suggests, take place on external sites instead of on your site. This also means that it is not as easy as on-page SEO as it is not all in your control.

Off-page SEO mainly involves link building.

Link Building Process:

Link building is the process of having other sites point to your site. Google sees these links as a sort of 'vote' saying that your site content is good enough to be linked to. Link building involves manually building links to your site either by submission, which is at your discretion, or by requesting other sites to link to you.

Link earning on the other hand involves naturally gaining links i.e. having sites link to you without asking for them. You get these links naturally over time when your business makes a name for itself and people want to talk about you on their site and link to your site.

You can check your backlinks using backlink checker tools such as Ahrefs or SEMrush. These are both paid tools but very accurate and useful. You can also check your competitors backlinks by inserting their site into the tool. This is very powerful information because it gives you an entire list of all of the sites linking to your competitors and you can try to get links for yourself from those sites too. It shows you who's talking about your competitors, what they're saying, where your competitors have been interviewed, where they have been guest posting etc.

100+ plus link building ideas:

1. **Resources:** Resources pages are pages with lists of links. They're all over the web and exist for practically every industry. You can find them by inserting your keywords into search strings, a list of which you'll find in the next chapter.

2. **Unlinked Brand Mentions:** There are many times when site owners talk about your brand but they don't link back. These are called unlinked brand mentions. The fact that they mentioned your business is great but not enough to send over traffic because there is no link. Not many people reading the article will put in the effort to copy your brand name and search it to find your site. A link back is required for traffic purposes and also for backlink purposes. Getting sites with unlinked brand mentions to you to link back is an easy link building method because since those sites are already talking about you, they don't mind linking back since all the work is already done and they already know about you. You can find such mentions at a scale in just a few minutes

using a few tools (tutorials are up on this and other topics in the Digiologist Marketing Course).

3. **Misspelled Mentions:** If there are more than a few ways to type your company name or even a few possible spelling mistakes, insert them into the tools to find unlinked mentions with the wrong company name as well. This should also be done for company name variations and short forms and also previous names incase you recently changed your name.

4. **URL Mentions:** Along with finding brand name mentions, it's also important to find URL mentions i.e. when sites use your site URL into their article instead of your brand name. Though this is less common, it's still important to go after. The URLs being referred to here are the ones not resulting in hyperlinks due to a missing http:// and so, not resulting in an actual link.

5. **Track Industry Term Mentions:** Create an alert for popular industry term mentions so you know which sites are talking about specific topics in your industry. It would be a better idea to track very particular terms that are detailed so you're not bombarded with alerts. Tracking such terms will bring up prospects of sites mentioning them and possible sites and pages you can get a link from by contributing in some way.

6. **Competitors Brand Mentions:** You can't exactly get a link for your competitors brand mention, but you can track your competitors

brand mentions to see where they are being linked from. Check out the sites where they're getting mentioned and try getting a link for your site from them too.

7. **Competitor Backlink Analysis:** You can use tools to get access to the entire backlink profile of your competitors. After getting a list of their backlinks, sort according to quality and see which of the sites you can possibly get a link from.

8. **Competitors Common Backlink Analysis:** Involves using a tool like Majestic SEO that can look into the backlinks of a few of your competitors and find the backlinks they all have in common. Finding the sites each of your competitors has in common allows you to go after the top sites first and is faster than individual competitor analysis.

9. **Get an Indirect Backlink From Your Competitor:** It is quite common that some of your competitors link to the same sites. Link Juice Thief (LJT) finds places where your competitors commonly link to. These sites are usually big authorities in your industry. The Link Juice Thief (LJT) has a similar results matrix to the Common Backlinks Tool (CBLT). In many cases, you will find that the pages your competitors link to are authoritative sites in your niche.

10. **Competitors Newest Links:** Very often, a quick reaction can mean the difference between success and failure. On the Internet, it is pretty similar. It is extremely important to be

aware of your competitor's activities. Link Alerts (LA) is a tool made to inform you about your new backlinks, but, apart from that, you can also use it to monitor your competitors. Not only will it help you find some new backlink opportunities, but it can also enable you to discover some new sources and techniques you could use in the future.

11. **Ranking Pages Backlink Analysis:** From an SEO perspective, all sites ranking above you in the search engines for your preferred keywords are competitors. Most business think of their competitors as the ones getting more business and this is mostly in the offline sense. The competitors referred to in point #10 are the companies you feel are your competitors in whichever sense, be it in terms of more business, popularity etc. From an SEO perspective, any site that ranks above you for a preferred keyword is your competitor. Take the exact pages that rank above you and get the backlinks pointing to those pages (not the entire domain, but actual pages) and see which ones you can get a link on for yourself.

12. **Guest Posting:** Guest posting involves writing articles for other blogs in your industry with a link back to your site. This allows those other sites to get good content, and you for you to get a link to your site and incoming traffic from the site. So a win-win situation for both. Guest posting is a very common link building technique. Some say it's dead, spammy and not safe. But if done right, it can add a lot of

value. What you need to keep in mind while guest posting is to post on the highest quality possible sites that are not spammy and are relevant. Relevancy is the key factor here. You don't want to guest post just for the sake of getting a link. Make value your top priority. Guest post on sites that are relevant to your industry i.e. sites that can send relevant traffic to your site that can possibly lead to sales. The most common approach to guest posting is simply reaching out to influential blog owners in your niche. It's a great idea but getting a guest post to go live on influential blogs is not always easy. These blogs are popular and so receive hundreds of outreach emails a day requesting to guest blog for them. Some of these blogs don't even accept guest posts and clearly state that. However, to get a higher response rate, it is a better idea to reach out to sites that are actually accepting guest posts. You can find these sites quickly using search strings (which have been explained in detail later on). There are also various guest posting communities like Post Joint (postjoint.com), Guestr (guestr.com), Blogger Link Up (bloggerlinkup.com), My Blog Guest (myblogguest.com) that list out sites in need of guest posts, industry wise. Another way to find guest post opportunities is to trace your competitors guest posts and seeing which sites they've written on by checking their backlinks. You can also trace the guest post path of top bloggers in your industry.

13. **Guest Posting Communities:** Guest posting communities such as Blog Dash, My Blog Guest, Blogger Link Up etc are all sites that have lists of blogs in different niches that are accepting guest posts so the step of site prospecting is not required to be done if guest posting through these communities. Some of these communities also allow putting a notice on them for either writers required for guest posting or sites required to guest post on.

14. **Reverse Guest Posting:** Reverse guest posting involves inviting guest bloggers to blog on your site instead of you on theirs and having them share and link to what their article on your site from their site.

15. **Private Blog Networks:** Private blog networks are a group of blogs created by the same individual for the purpose of having a group of sites to get links from to the main site. You can either create your own PBN to link to your main site or purchase a link package from a PBN owner.

16. **Get Students to Blog on University Blogs:** University and college students have access to the institutions blog portal and can be hired to do an article on your business or drop a link to your site in an already written relevant article.

17. **Sponsored Posts:** Involves sponsoring the publication of a guest post on a blog i.e. a paid guest post placement.

18. **Paid Links:** Can either be a sponsored guest post or a paid text link.

19. **Interlinking:** Interlinking is not offsite but can still add a lot of value and help in ranking. It involves linking your sites internal pages to each other. Since the links are coming from your site, you have the authority to choose their location and anchor text so take advantage of that. You can link from your highest ranking and most visited pages to pages you want to boost, to your ranking pages to help increase their ranking further or to important landing pages. There are many choices, split test them and see what works.

20. **Broken Link Building:** There are many sites out there linking out to broken pages that are either to sites that were shut down or pages that just don't exist anymore. You can find these pages at scale for sites in your industry and inform the webmasters and request your link to be replaced in place.

21. **Competitors 404s:** Find out your competitors 404s and who links to them and ask them to link to yourself instead.

22. **Reclaim Links Pointing to 404 Pages:** If you've been making some site changes recently and deleted or moved some pages and now have a few missing pages a.k.a 404s, check to see if there are any links pointing to them and have them changed to existing and more updated pages on your site instead.

23. **Reclaim External Profile Link Pages:** People will link to you if they like your product without you even requesting a link. But at times, such naturally earned links can be pointed to your

social profiles instead of your website. A lot of times people link to Twitter the most and while getting a link to your Twitter is great, it's a good idea to reclaim links to your social profiles to your website instead. At times you can even keep the link to your social profile because the webmasters just needs to add a link to your site in addition.

24. **Home Page Links to Deeper Pages:** This isn't a strategy to gain new links but is still useful. You can conduct a backlink analysis of your site and see if there are too many incoming links to the home page and contact those sites to point those already existing links to deeper and more relevant pages for a more mixed link portfolio.

25. **Nofollow to Dofollow:** This isn't a strategy to gain new links but is still useful. You can conduct a backlink analysis of your site and see if there are too many incoming no-follow links to the home page and contact those sites to change them to do-follow so link juice can pass. Don't go overboard with this because it's a good idea to have some no-follow links as well for a natural link portfolio. But if any high authority sites have provided your site with no-follow links, it doesn't hurt to ask them to change them.

26. **Forum Commenting:** Forum link building is similar to Q and A sites. Forums are like online groups. They're created for a specific industry where people post threads to ask questions, ask for opinions, or simply just discuss a

particular topic. You can become a member of a few of the main forums from your industry and join in on the conversations taking place. Getting links from the forum threads is not always possible in the beginning since the admins are strict about it. But once you gain a reputation by becoming a frequent poster, you can start dropping links. Comment on popular threads or ones you think will gain popularity soon and try linking your answer back to your business in some or the other way. Offer the thread poster help or a valuable opinion and let them know they can visit your site for more information. The thread poster and also the hundreds, if not thousands of people viewing the thread will read your answer.

27. **Forum Profiles:** Registering for forums allows each user to create a forum profile which is like a social media profile. Each forum profile has an about section and a section to add your website which should be filled.

28. **Blog Commenting:** This is something a lot of people do naturally. We all read many blog posts a day to do our share of industry reading. Why not leave a comment after reading while you're on the page? Try not to leave spammy links in every comment though. Most commenting systems such as Disqus let users profiles link to their sites, so you end up getting a link that way. You can provide a valuable point not discussed in the article or give your opinion so it stands out and gets noticed by people reading the comments. We often

underestimate the number of people who read comments on an article and because of that blog commenting is often overlooked, but give it a try.

29. **Q & A Sites:** These links aren't the highest quality for backlink purposes but they can be huge for increasing incoming traffic. Q and A sites like Yahoo Answers, Quora etc. get a large number of hits a month so build a presence there. Find questions related to your industry that have been asked and answer them. You answer the question and so help someone, end up being perceived as the expert and get a link back to your site. If you provide value to others through helpful answers, they will make their way to your site and your traffic (and hopefully leads) will increase. A sneaky little trick is to post a question yourself and answer it yourself as well. But use different accounts for that so it looks natural ofcourse. This Q and A thread may be made up but it will still be valuable to the others reading it as they're searching for answer to that question.

30. **Link Reclamation:** Some of the links you previously built or earned may go missing with time. This could be due to pages removed from the sites of previous linkers or they could go lost during their site redesign processes. You can always reach out to them and ask for a link again in some way. You don't have to manually keep a check on this. Upload all links built and earned into Raven Tools and it will

automatically notify you each time a link is removed.

31. **Link Re-purposing:** This isn't a technique to build new fresh links, but rather repurpose old ones. You may have most of your link pointing to your home page or even an old landing page that might not even exist anymore. You can reach out to the site owners linking to you and have them link to a different page instead that is a more important internal page. It's a good idea to have your links pointing to your home page as well as deeper internal pages. But if too many of them point to your home page, go for some diversity and request some of them to be changed.

32. **Anchor Text Re-purposing:** Changing 'click here', 'site' anchor texts to more descriptive ones.

33. **Get Local Library Links:** Libraries usually have a link page on their site to act as a resource for the general public as a compilation of professionals from different industries. Check out your local library's website and see if you can get listed on it.

34. **Expired Domain Link Building:** Sites become expired and shut down all the time. You can take advantage of that and either purchase those domains and redirect to your site (more info on that in point #35) or simply check their backlinks and request the sites linking to them to link to you instead. This only works and is worth doing if the expired sites are in the same industry as you. It can work with sites in

adjacent industries as well. These links are also easy to get because the site owners are informed they're linking to expired domains so they're interested in removing the link immediately and mostly open to replacing it with your link in exchange for the help.

35. **Moved Sites:** Some businesses close or move to other sites, leaving their old site behind and expired. Register any such sites from your industry that have a good backlink profile and use them to your advantage. You can either use those domains for building a site and linking to yourself from it, or simply redirecting it to a relevant page on your site.

36. **Non-existent Service Pages:** Find pages or sites that used to offer a service but no longer do and have their backlinks pointed to your site instead. Businesses get shut down or have some of their products/services removed all the time. If you find out about something shut down in your industry and the particular page or site that used to represent it has a good number of backlinks, inform the site owners they're linking to a removed product/service and have them replace the link to your existing product instead.

37. **Expired Blogspot Blogs with Good Backlinks:** Blogspot is a blogging platform providing free hosting. It uses a .blogspot domain that looks something like: www.example.blogspot.com. The great thing about blogspot is that when a user shuts their blog, their blogspot address is available for

anyone to register. And it's free. You can take advantage of that by registering shut down blogpost blog addresses that had some good backlinks.

38. **Find Sites With Spammy Links:** Similar method to malware and broken links, find sites in your industry with spammy backlinks using a backlink checker and inform them about it.

39. **Find Sites With Malware:** Malware is a hostile software causing viruses and computer damage. Using tools, find sites with malware and contact the owners and let them know about it. This puts you in their good books and is more likely to get you a link. This is similar to broken link building.

40. **Get your own Wikipedia Page:** If you've built enough authority, get yourself a Wikipedia page. Just have someone else write it for you so it looks natural and is unbiased.

41. **Content Gaps:** Filling content gaps involves improving the content on topics in your industry on other sites. There's plenty of content out there that is incomplete and could just use a few additions to improve it. You being the industry expert can reach out to those sites with additional information and be quoted as a source or score yourself a link in some other way such as through a guest article or on their blogroll.

42. **Content Updating:** Involves updating old and outdated content on topics in your industry on other sites. You can reach out to those sites with the latest up to date information on the

subject and be quoted as a source or score yourself a link in some other way such as through a guest article or on their blogroll.

43. **Content Improvement:** Find a piece of content that has a ton of links. Create a better version of it. Alert the sites linking to it that you've built a better piece of content.

44. **Content Curation:** Content curation involves finding the best content on the web, compiling it and sharing it with your network. There are various sites you can use for this, one of them being Scoop.it. Create an account on them and post curated content regularly to build a following. Once you've created a following, you then have access to a network of people interested in your industry that you can post your content to whenever you need to.

45. **Link Poaching:** Link poaching involves having your competitors backlinks replaced to links pointing to your site instead. It's sneaky and even a little mean. But if you can provide sites that are linking to your competitors sites with better content to link to on your site instead and replace the links, just think of it as adding more value to those sites for their readers. Be careful about this though. You may not want to have all of your competitors links replaced and start a war.

46. **Content Link Replacements:** This is similar to link poaching, except that it doesn't involve stealing your competitors links but just links to other content. Find content in your industry that ranks well and you have a substitute for on

your blog, get a list of its backlinks, reach out to the sites linking to that content and let them know that you have a similar article that is a better and a more updated version that they can link to instead. You mainly just find content that is ranking, make it better and ask people linking to it to link to your updated and better content.

47. **Content Syndication:** Involves signing up for a syndication service or manually uploading your blog content to third party sites such as web 2.0s, press release sites, article directories etc to increase the exposure and readership of it.

48. **Create Great Content and Ask for Links:** One of the simplest ways of link building is to just create linkable content. Create assets that are link worthy. This could be in the form of eBooks, whitepapers, infographics, guides, market research studies/ surveys or just blog articles. It doesn't have to be super fancy and lengthy. Just provide value and make it better than your competitors so people see why they should link to you.

49. **Dead Content Recreation:** This involves offering to update old content out there on other sites that is outdated. Find content from your industry that was written a few or many years ago, reach out to the webmasters and offer to give them an updated version. This works well not only for old content, but also content on different strategies/ techniques/technologies from your industry that

are now obsolete and replaced with something more updated.

50. **Link Roundups:** These are compilations of great links on a certain topic you can put together on your blog. These can be lists of great articles that recently came up in your industry or links to niche influencers sites. After you're done publishing your roundup, contact the people linked to in it. They will appreciate the mention and most will either link back to your roundup article or at least socially share it.

51. **Check Copyscape for Copied Content:** Everything that you put out on the web has chances of being stolen. Keep a check on which of your content gets copied and posted on other sites. If you're sensitive about it you can just ask those site owners to remove the content. But if you're more concerned with getting a link, reach out to the sites and ask for your site to be linked to and quoted as the source of that content. Ideally you don't want entire articles of yours to be posted elsewhere as Google treats it as duplicate content and it's not favored. So if possible, try to have portions of the original content used instead of the entire article.

52. **Content Available for Reuse:** Available for re-use by linking back.

53. **Add A Snippet Feature to Your Content:** Uploading your content online will attract people stealing your content no matter what. People will right click and save and republish elsewhere. A trick to try to get a link while they

do that is adding snippets to your content. That way, along with picking up your content, the person also copies a link back (and also a short summary) to your site along with it.

54. **Contact People Using Your Images:** Similar to using Copyscape to check people using your content, use image source checker tools like Tineye to find people who have used your images without permission. If you're sensitive about it, you can ask them to remove the images but if you want a link, you can have them add a link back to you under the image and quote you as the source for the image.

55. **Get Image Hotlinkers to Link to You:** Image hotlinking involves displaying images on your site that belong to another site and are displayed by linking to the image on the other site without having to save and upload the image. It is also referred to as inline linking. When the website with the hotlinked image is opened, the image is displayed but it is actually loaded from the site where it is originally located. Note that this also uses up more bandwidth from your site so if you want to prevent that, you can disable hotlinking altogether. If you're okay with giving up a bit of bandwidth in exchange for backlinks from hotlinkers, you need to enable a script. This can be done easily using a plugin.

56. **Offer Images to be Used With Credit:** In addition to providing image embed codes and getting credit from those using your images without permission, it's a good idea to simply

offer your images for use as well. When you offer them, more people will know they're available for use and they are more likely to end up on sites and so, more links obtained. Just put giving credit through a link back as the source as the criteria for being allowed to use your images.

57. **Embed Codes (Images, Content, Videos):** Similar to using snippets for content, add image embed code options under every image. This will give people the option of using the images on their site using the embed code instead of saving and uploading them. This also straight away gives them permission and encourages them to use the images. You automatically get a link back from the embed codes used and you can set that up by creating custom codes through Embedly (www. embed.ly).

58. **Reverse Image Searches:** Similar to finding sites that have copied your content, it involves finding sites that have used your images without permission using a tool like TinEye. You can either have those sites remove the images or turn it into a link building opportunity and ask those sites to link to you and give you credit by listing your site as the source of the image.

59. **Ask for Links from Partners and Vendors:** Have vendors you frequently purchase from? You've already built the relationship so leverage it and get a link out of it. You can ask to be places on their 'friends page' if they have

one or offer to write them a testimonial for their site.

60. **Ask People You Know for a Link:** People you know refers to your friends. Think about all the friends you have and all the contacts you've built through networking that have their own businesses whose sites you can get a link from.

61. **Previous Linkers:** Check your backlinks and see if any previous linkers are interested in linking to your site again.

62. **Ask Your Customers:** Ask your best customers which business they're in and see if getting a link from them is possible. Often times your customers have their own business too and can give you a link if relevant.

63. **Transcribe Videos:** Transcribing videos involves making a transcript of the content of the video i.e. producing a written version of the videos content. Find YouTube videos in your industry that have done well, contact the owner and ask them if they'd like you to transcribe the video so they can use the written version of the video on their blog. This would be useful to them because the written version of the video as a blog article would also have chances of doing well. Also, it is something that's easy for you to produce and can be done from Fiverr and relevant websites for just a few bucks. Transcribing other site owner's videos is a way to get links by helping others. It's a fast way of relationship building that gets you links back in return some or the other way.

64. **Blog Post Translation:** If your blog is in English, have some of your blog posts shared on other sites in other countries in other languages after translation. Some popular language choices other than English would be Mandarin and Spanish, which are the most spoken languages globally before English. This can be like a guest article, except that you're not writing new content but just repurposing old content and making it new through translation. This is great for businesses that have their product/service available worldwide so they can target audiences in other countries.

65. **Translating Content:** Similar to transcribing content, translating content produces another version of the same content as well. Offer to translate other people's popular blog posts into other languages such as from English to Mandarin, Spanish etc., so they can avail benefit from those markets as well. Again, this is a strategy of link building involving helping others to build relationships that can be used to get links in return.

66. **Associations/Organizations:** Get a link from associations or organizations in your industry you're a part of or join them.

67. **Awards:** Get a link from sites of committees or organizations your business got awards from in the past.

68. **Blog Badge:** Create a blog badge and inform your readers. Your most loyal readers will share it on their sites and link back to you.

69. **Blog Carnival:** Blog carnivals are like link submission parties, except that the link needs to be to an article. Blog carnivals, which are sometimes also called blog parties, have a theme or topic announced before hand and ask for bloggers to submit articles links talking about that topic. If you participate and submit a link to your article on that topic, you get an immediate link.

70. **Blog Incubation:** Blog incubation involves starting your own blogs to get links from. This refers to blogs separate from your main site. These are like mini blogs you make just for the sake of linking to yourself from. Keep them on topics related to your industry so the links built are relevant.

71. **Blogrolls:** Blogrolls are lists of blog owners favourite blogs. They're a way of listing out all the blogs they read and recommend to their readers. While it may be tough to get on someone's blogroll without knowing them at first, it's a good idea to build a relationship and introduce them to your blog so they see the value in adding it to their roll.

72. **Classified Ads:** You can also get links from online classified sites such as Craigslist and Kijiji. If you're from a larger, more well known company, you may not want to do this to keep up your brand image but if you're just starting out and like the sound of the idea then go for it.

73. **Job Postings:** Have an open position? Many times business owners rely on filling positions through referrals and don't post job openings

online. It's a good idea to take advantage of the opening and post it on high traffic job sites like Monster, Workopolis etc. You get a link and also get more applicants.

74. **Contest/Giveaway on Other Bloggers Sites:** In addition to giving away your product/service on your site, offer to give it as a prize for other bloggers giveaways with a rule for entry being either sharing your site socially or linking back to your site through a blog post. This way, all the participants will link back to your site in order to get an entry to the contest and so you end up getting multiple links.

75. **Create Industry Tools:** Industry tools like widgets and calculators are great linkbait. They are helpful to people and so get shared and linked to easily and frequently.

76. **Display Ads:** Display ads through banners on other sites get you an immediate link. While this may be a short-term image link, it's still worth experimenting with. This can allow you get a link on some of the best blogs in your industry and for a much lower price than if you directly asked them for a link and they wanted it to be a paid transaction. This is also really good for increasing traffic and leads.

77. **Fixing Grammar/Spelling:** Grammar or spelling mistakes can be found at scale using tools so don't worry about spending hours manually looking for mistakes. Have the tool search for any errors in popular articles from your industry and if you find any errors, let the site owner know so they can correct them.

They'll appreciate your help and it will be easier for you to get a link in some way from their site then from a guest post, resource page, blogroll etc. because you've helped them and built the relationship.

78. **Get Interviewed:** Offer yourself for interviews. You can reach out to industry bloggers and offer to be interviewed or find interview opportunities through PR sites. You can also follow the interview path of your competitors to see which sites they've been interviewed on and try to score an interview for yourself there as well. All this is easier to accomplish if you've developed a bit of a following.

79. **Interview Journalists Who Cover Your Niche:** Similar to reverse guest posting, interview influential bloggers on your site instead of you being interviewed on theirs. They will appreciate it and in most cases, share a link to it on their site.

80. **Getting Trackbacks:** When you link to other bloggers from your blog articles and source them as relevant blog posts or references, you can fill their link in the trackback section. This then leaves a trackback (also called pingback) on the other bloggers article in the comments section as a link and short summary to your article. These may not always appear instantly though as some bloggers like to manually approve them. But either way, they're great for relationship building.

81. **Giving Trackbacks:** Giving trackbacks is important as well as sites like to link to sites

that give out trackbacks so they can benefit from linking to you. This makes sites want to link to you.

82. **Give Product/Service for Review:** Give your product or offer your service to influential bloggers to try out and review on their end. This helps get the word out and backlinks.

83. **Give Products/Service Away in a Giveaway:** Give away your product or service in a giveaway or contest on your site. You can set sharing your site socially or writing a blog post about an industry topic with a link to your site at the bottom as the rules for entry. This way, all the participants will link back to your site in order to get an entry to the contest and so you end up getting multiple links.

84. **Best Blogs List:** Also known as 'blogrolls', this is a list of your favourite blogs from the industry and can also be made as a list of your favorite tools, softwares etc. You can then reach out to the people listed and let them know they've been mentioned and get links in the same way as monthly/weekly 'best of' lists mentioned in the previous point would get you. Another method is to reach out to sites that have their own blogrolls and request to be listed on them.

85. **Monthly/Weekly 'Best of' List:** Create an ongoing 'best of' list either each week or month where you link to the best articles or overall blogs from your industry by compiling them into a list. This is like a round up and similar to article round ups that are one question interview style, except that with this strategy

you're creating a list style compilation of your favorite links. After creating and publishing it, reach out to the people you mentioned in it and let them know you gave them a shoutout on your site. This will allow you to build a relationship with them easier and at times they will link back to the list they've been mentioned in or return the love some other way.

86. **Local Links:** It's important to search for local link opportunities while implementing different link building opportunities such as looking for local directories and placing guest posts on local blogs etc.

87. **Offer a Scholarship:** Offer a scholarship to students from different universities having writing an essay as the criteria for entry. The students will post their essay on their blog (and create blogs incase they don't have one) and link to your site as the source of the scholarship as the rule for entry.

88. **Offer Student Discounts:** Offering student discounts is a great way to get links from university and college sites, backlinks from which are considered high in value.

89. **Phone Based Link Building:** Not exactly a link building method but this idea works extremely well. When you request for a link through a phone call rather than an email, it is a lot easier make the relationship and get the link as you can be more personable and communicate better over phone. It's not possible to pick up the phone for each link

you're trying to build so do this for the top sites you're trying to get a link from.

90. **Sponsor Events:** Build relationships by sponsoring local events. The event sponsors are shown on the event site and usually linked to.

91. **Volunteering:** Volunteer to help out local charities, NGOs, organizations. This helps build relationships and it is easier getting links with those relationships. Most such organizations have a members page on their site which they use to link to participating companies.

92. **Donations:** Through donations you build relationships and look good in the community. Philanthropy work is always appreciated. Organizations that accept donations usually have a donators list on their site where you can have yourself added and linked to after giving the donation. A good idea would be search before hand which sites offer this.

93. **PR Commenting:** Make an account on PR commenting sites like HARO (Help a Reporter Out) and Response Source. These sites have a lot of journalists sign up that are looking for opinions from specialists in different fields. You get all of the questions/topics that replies are required for from journalists and you can answer the ones related to your industry. If the journalist finds your content useful, they use it in their article and quote you and link back to your site. This is great for backlinks and excellent for traffic. At times you can get links

from very reputable sites such as Huffington Post, Forbes etc. that is otherwise quite difficult.

94. **Quotes:** Find quotes from popular (but not very popular) influencers from your industry and use their quotes in articles on your site and let them know you mentioned them. Don't do this with very popular personalities though since it's difficult to contact them.

Earning links naturally by uploading link bait (high quality content worth linking to that is created to attract links) is better than link building as you don't have to ask for the links as they're organic and acquired naturally as the other person wants to link to your content. Below are some link earning methods:

95. **Blog:** Setting up a business blog on your site is bound to get you more links rather than not having one. The more content you publish, the more content other sites have to possibly link to.

96. **Infoanimations:** Infoanimations are short animated videos. They're usually a few minutes long only and are made with the same goal infographics are made with: to explain complex topics in an easier way. These again are something that not everyone is doing and have better chances of going viral.

97. **Memes:** Memes may not be suitable for all businesses but if your business isn't too formal,

give memes a try instead in addition to other graphics like infographics.

98. **Infographics:** Though infographics and guest posts as strategies have been exhausted in the past, they still work, provided you do them right. Have a few infographics designed each year that are high quality and unique so they're shareable and stand out from all the other infographics out there so people want to share them. After having them designed reach out to site owners and allow them to use the graphics on their site with a link back.

99. **Comics:** Again, not suitable for all businesses but worth a try. If done well, they have chances of going viral and they're definitely unique and not something everyone is doing.

100. **Instructional Gifs:** Instructional gifs are a very new strategy. Hardly anyone is doing them so it's a great time to jump on board. Instructional gifs are like screencast videos, except much shorter like 15- 20 seconds long. Though you can't explain in-depth and do an entire strategy tutorial, you can make these about little hacks and make multiple of them that all flow together as single steps to complete one large task.

101. **Case Studies:** A study about a topic that has been done over time with research and facts.

102. **Research Papers:** A study on a topic containing extensive research.

103. **Whitepapers:** An in-depth report created to educate the reader on the topic.

104.   **Guides:** Are all in one pieces of lengthy content that explain a topic in-depth.

105.   **Glossary:** A list of terms related to an industry and their definitions.

106.   **Lists:** Can be a list of anything related to an industry that is useful. For example, in SEO, a list of tools would be helpful.

107.   **Checklists:** A checklist can be a list of items to not forget or things to complete. For example, in SEO a list of places on-page to place keywords would make a helpful checklist.

108.   **Podcasts:** A recording or audio file on a particular topic and these are usually episodes. They're like audio presentations of articles.

109.   **Webinars:** Online seminars i.e. live seminars that take place on the web and hence the name webinar.

Directory link building involves submitting your site to relevant online directories such as business directories, industry specific directories, local directories etc. Submission link building involves submitting your assets such as images, videos, slides etc to submission sites around those materials. Below are some directory and submission link building ideas:

110.   **1-800 Directories**
111.   **Alumni Directories**
112.   **App Directories**
113.   **Article Submissions**
114.   **Audio Sharing Sites**
115.   **Blog URL Directories**

116. **Business Card Directories**
117. **Business Directories**
118. **Coupon Sites**
119. **CSS Galleries**
120. **Document Sharing**
121. **eBook directories**
122. **Image Submission**
123. **Infoanimation Submissions**
124. **Infographic submissions**
125. **Logo Gallery Directories**
126. **PDF Submisisons**
127. **Podcast Directories**
128. **Profile Directories**
129. **RSS irectories**
130. **Slide Submissions**
131. **Tool, Plugin and Widget Directories**
132. **Video Submissions**
133. **Webinar Directories**
134. **Reciprocal Link Building:** Make a deal and link to relevant sites to have them link back to you. This basically involves trading links. Do this sparingly and with caution though.
135. **Three Way Links:** A linking system that takes place between 3 sites where site A links to site B, site B links to site C and site C links to site A.
136. **Link Wheels:** A group of sites that link to each other in a strategic manner. For example, in the case of 6 sites, namely. A, B, C, D, E and F. With A being the main site, then B links to C, C links to D, D links to E, E links to F, F links to B and B links to A, thereby completing the wheel.

137.   Tiered Link Building (Link Pyramid): A tiered link building approach where a set of tier 1 or 'base links' point to the main site, a set of tier 2 or middle links point to the tier 1 links and a set of tier 3 links which are usually low in quality but high in number, point to the tier 2 links.

138.   **Testimonials:** Reach out to the sites of products/ services you regularly use for your business and offer to provide a testimonial for their site. They'll not only use it and give you a link back from it to your site, but also appreciate it and easily accept it.

139.   **Web 2.0:** This involves creating a presence on web 2.0 sites like Tumblr, Blogger, Wordpress etc. Web 2.0 sites are like free blogging platforms. You can put relevant content on them by outsourcing articles or through article spinning. Use a good quality paid article spinning tool so it results in articles that are completely different from the ones you input into it and it gives you fresh readable content. Don't go for article scraping though. Once you've built up authority and a readership on your web 2.0 properties, you can start adding links to them pointing to your main site. These links will be relevant and all in your control so you get to choose their location, anchor text etc and since the articles are spun content, you do all this through minimal effort.

140.   **Adjacent Markets:** Although there are numerous link building strategies and opportunities, there will come a time when

you'll exhaust your opportunities. When you do, it's good idea to look into opportunties related to adjacent markets i.e. industries that function alongside your industry as a cross dependance on one another but not in competition. For example, pens and papers. They're both different products and production industries, not competitors but are required by one another.

141. **Press Releases:** A statement or article containing news, updates and information that is supplied to online news portals. Anytime you make any site changes, updates, release new products, you should create and send off a press release and insert a link to your site.

142. **Alumni Profiles:** If you went to college or university, it's a good idea to join the alumni team and be given the opportunity to create a profile on the site of the institution, resulting in a .edu link.

I haven't suggested individual sites in this link building ideas list but the below 3 sites are important ones:

143. **Gov Chamber of Commerce:** Every country's government has a website which usually lists businesses in that country and are a high authority site to get a link from by creating a profile.

144. **Dmoz:** The oldest and most authoritative directory online.

145. **BBB:** Stands for Better Business Bureau and is the top business directory.

146. **Citations:** An online reference and display of your company name, address and phone number (NAP) in that particular order. Similar to link building, citations should be placed across various external sites for improving local rankings. While building citations (which are usually placed on directories) it is easy and advised to get a link by placing the link on the same page as well.

147. **Discount Promotions:** Run a discount promotion and get listed in deal websites (i.e. redflagdeals.com in Canada).

148. **Social Bookmarking:** Webpages bookmarked on social bookmarking sites, which search engines see as quality content and a backlink.

149. **Mini Sites:** A site with a keyword rich domain linking to the main site and created to rank in search engines along with the mini site in order to capture multiple top spots in the SERPs.

Hold on...

You made it so far into this book! I'm so glad you're enjoying it!

Want to take your learning even further?

Check out my SEO Course at Digiologist.com

Course available at https://goo.gl/C43oMO

Course Details:

- 4.5 Hours of video tutorials
- 52 video lessons
- Lifetime Access
- Continually Updated

I have a special coupon code for my valuable readers only!

Use the coupon code 'Amazon' for 75% off.

Course syllabus and reviews listed at the end of this book.

Importance of Link Anchor Text

Anchor text is the visible clickable text on a link. In simple words, anchor text is the word or group of words that are clickable that open a link when you can click on them. The anchor text of the links you build are important and powerful. Having your targeted keywords as the anchor text of the links to your site helps you rank for those keywords. Google takes the anchor text to be the description of the link, and thus, the description of the pages content, thereby increasing your chances of ranking for such terms. Although anchor text is powerful, it can also have a negative effect if exact anchor texts are used repeatedly for many links. To avoid overuse of specific keywords as anchor text, use different keywords or variations of your main keyword. Of course when you're building links, choosing the anchor text is at the discretion of the person giving you the link so your choice of anchor text is not always guaranteed and the most you can do is simply request it. Another thing to keep in mind is to have a good mix of branded links, naked links and anchor text links. Branded links use your business name as the anchor text and naked links are just links without any anchor texts. This makes your anchor text portfolio appear natural. It's also good to have a mixture of pages to which links point. It is natural to have the majority of your backlinks point to your home page because most times the home page is the most relevant page to represent the brand overall and most naturally earned links are pointed to the home page.

But because home page links are common, try gaining links to deeper internal pages wherever possible.

Nofollow vs. Dofollow:

Not all links are created equal. A link can either be dofollow or nofollow. A dofollow link passes link value and a nofollow link doesn't and they are not followed or considered by search engines. In short, a nofollow link has no value in terms of SEO. But that doesn't mean they're completely useless. They are still visible to the readers and bring in traffic. It's also a good idea to have a link portfolio containing a mixture of dofollow and nofollow links, as it appears more natural. The decision of whether a link is to be dofollow or nofollow is made by the site owner who creates the link. You can check whether a link is dofollow or nofollow using a browser add on called Mozbar (moz.com/tools/seo-toolbar). It automatically highlights all dofollow and nofollow links on a page.

What Makes a Good Link:

1. From a site with content relevant to your niche
2. From a site with high metrics (DA, PA, PR)*
3. Dofollow
4. Relevant anchor text
5. From an authoritative site with a good TLD
6. High on-page social shares

*The metrics referred to above are DA i.e. domain

authority, PA i.e. page authority and PR i.e. page-rank. These are all website metrics that give a number denoting the power of the domain in the case of DA and the power of the page in case of PA and PR. You can check these metrics for sites from using URL Profiler (urlprofiler.com) or Netpeak Checker (netpeak.net/software/netpeak-checker).

Outreach Email Do's and Don'ts

While building links, in many cases to get a link you will have to reach out to people and request it. These people are the webmasters get hundreds of emails a day with requests such as for being added to a resource page on their site, to be allowed to submit a guest post etc. Your email has to stand out and so it's not rejected. Your subject line is the first thing the webmaster sees so make it attractive enough so they actually open your email. A small part of the beginning of your email is also visible to them before they actually even open your email so make that part interesting too. Try sending emails from a personal name rather than using the company name, as people are more likely to open it then. It's important to keep it short and to explain the value that they're getting as well.

Outreach Email Tips:

While searching for the contact information of prospects you want a link from, you'll notice that the email given on the website about page is usually a generic email such as info@example.com or contact@example.com and mostly not for a specific person. If you know the name of the person you want to contact, you can usually get their name through a Google search.

If you don't know who you want to contact but are looking for the email of anyone that works there over contacting a generic email, type in the website with .com and add in the term 'email' and search. This search will look for emails with that sites domain name for you. For example, if you're looking for all possible emails associated with a website, you need to insert the following into Google:

example.com email

If you were trying to find my email you'd type in:

digiologist.com email

It will then pull out all pages not just on that site but other sites as well with emails using the example.com domain. While you're on the search page, press CTRL + F (or Command + F for MAC users) and type in @. It will then highlight all @ symbols, and thus, highlight all the emails it found making it easier for you to spot them and you'll get a list of all emails with that site on one page.

To see if emails you're sending are being opened, get Yesware (yesware.com). You can also save a significant amount of time and effort by sending emails in bulk through a mail merge instead of sending each email one by one. For that, just make a template that can be used for all the emails and insert a simple script in place of terms that need to be changed such as name, company name etc. It will then pull those terms from the sheet automatically and customize and send each email. You can send these emails off through a list created in Google spreadsheets using the Yet Another Mail Merge add on. Save time by scheduling emails and schedule them for days and times with higher open rates (weekdays and earlier in the day). Another important and popular software for link building is Buzzstream (buzzstream.com) which helps find contact information, conduct outreach, build databases of people to contact etc.

Link Earning Strategies

The strategies mentioned above are link building strategies. But what every marketer should aim for is link earning. Link earning is the automatic acquisition of backlinks without manually building them. It's work that automatically happens for you. It is when people naturally link to your content without you having to ask them to do so.

When and why do people do this? Link earning is possible when your content provides people value. In addition to that it is also important that your content ranks and is shared socially so people find it.

Here are some ideas for different kinds of content you can generate for your blog to serve as link bait that people find value form and link to naturally over time:

1. Glossary
2. Resource Pages
3. Interviews of Influencers
4. Epic Content: articles
5. Evergreen content
6. EBooks
7. Whitepapers
8. Research Papers
9. Market Studies
10. Infographics
11. Memes
12. Comics
13. Infoanimations
14. Videos
15. Monthly/Weekly 'Best of' Round Up List
16. Best Blogs List:
17. Quotes
18. Coming up with a new term
19. Great images
20. Gifs
21. Tools
22. Widgets
23. Softwares
24. Offer free downloadable assets
25. Podcast
26. Recorded webinars
27. Powerpoint Slides

28. Quizzes
29. Reader submitted queries/requests

You don't have to create all of the above. Just create whatever valuable content you can that is shareable.

Creating and Using Search Strings:

Search strings are a combination of keywords, characters and modifiers that make conducting more detailed searches a lot easier. They play an important role for searching for link opportunities.

Most people conduct searches in search engines by just inputting normal keyword combinations. When you're searching for something very specific and only want particular results, using search strings can help significantly. They're excellent for finding link building opportunities.

As mentioned above, search strings contain modifiers that in a way let the search engine know what it is you're searching for and also what you're not searching for i.e. what to exclude from the results.

Here are some modifiers you can add to your keywords to create search strings to conduct very specific and detailed searches:

1. " "

The quotation marks modifier yields exact results

based on whatever is inserted in the quotations. Whether you insert the entire search phrase into the quotes or a just a part of it, whatever it encloses is what the search engine is told to search for exactly as an exact match of the word(s).

Whatever part of the keyphrase lies outside the quotation marks may or may not be part of the search results (though it being a part of them is aimed for) but the words within the quotations are exactly matched in the search results.

Eg. Let's say you were to search the name John Jon. You could search the name like you normally would by inputting it as: John Jon into a search engine like Google like most people would. That would give you only some accurate results. It will give you some results by combining the two together as Johnjon, some with only John or Jon but not both and some with either of them but with a different first and last name.

If you add quotes to the name and search as: "John Jon", it gives you only John Jon in the results and exactly in the same order as written with a space and the same spelling. That's how the quotations modifier works. It gives you results containing the exact match of the keyword(s) inserted in quotes. Just a small addition can change the search results entirely and help you save a lot of time.

2. **AND**

The AND modifier can be used to combine two keyphrases to ensure both of them are part of the search results.

Eg. You want to adopt a pet and are confused between a cat or a dog so you're searching for cat and dog shelters. If you simply insert the term 'cat and dog shelter' you'll end up getting results for either of the two in both cases but rarely for both cats and dogs both. Instead, you need to search using: "cat" AND "dog" shelter Toronto. Using the quotes is important here.

Eg. You want to search for a person named Jane Doe who is a lawyer. If you simply search for Jane Doe lawyer, you'll get some pages that either have Jane Doe on the page or the term lawyer on the page, but not both on the same page. Use the search string "Jane Doe" AND "lawyer" instead and you'll get both of the terms on the same page and so, more relevant results.

3. −

The minus sign which is called the subtract modifier excludes any word(s) you don't want to be part of the search results.

Eg. If you're looking for furniture, let's say a sofa in Toronto but you're mostly getting back results from Kijiji and Craigslist which are sites you're not interested in buying from, you can use the following search string: buy sofa in Toronto -Kijiji -Craigslist

Insert the above into Google and it will remove all results from Kijiji and Craigslist. If you only search for 'buy sofa in Toronto', you'll get a lot of results from Kijiji and Craigslist. So using the subtract modifier helps in removing them.

4. OR

Used to get search results for either of multiple terms - either of two or more keyphrases but not necessarily all of them.

Eg. You want to search for gold jewellery but there are many ways of spelling jewellery based on location such as jewelery, jewellery, jewelry etc. Instead of searching three times, just search:

"gold" jewellery OR jewelry OR jewelery.

Since the term gold is the common one here, it needs to be in quotes.

5. Inurl:

Looks for presence of the keywords you're searching in the URLs of different sites rather than the content. Search:

Inurl:Barack Obama

It will then give back results with Barack Obama in the URL of the page.

6. **Intitle:**

Looks for pages with the keyphrase in the page title. Search:

Intitle:Barack Obama

It will then give back results with Barack Obama in the title of the page. You can also search

Intext:Barack Obama

It will then give back results with Barack Obama in the text (content body part) of the page.

7. **Related:**

It returns related results and sites similar to the keyword used. Search:

Related:reddit.com

It will then give back sites relevant to Reddit.

8. **Link:**

Acts as a backlink checker and finds pages linking to the URL inputted.

9. Site:example.com

Allows you to search anything within a particular site. So it yields search results from that one particular site only instead of from all sites across the web. Just put whatever you're searching for after the site address.

Eg. While searching the Digiologist site, you want to search for articles on link building, to search the entire site for link building articles you'd search:

Site:digiologist.com link building

After the .com part, leave a space and enter whatever it is you're searching for.

The above are just some of the main modifiers, but not all.

Using different modifiers together to create search strings:

Here are some examples of search strings using modifiers:

Example: Suppose you're in the health industry and you'd like to guest post on other sites for building links to your site.

The search string you'd use to find guest posting opportunities in the health industry:

health "guest post" OR "guest author" OR "guest blogger"

Example: Suppose you're a personal injury lawyer and want to make donations on behalf of your business to brain injury not for profits with the aim of being featured on the sites that you donated to.

You'd search for donation opportunities using:

"brain injury" donate OR make donation OR donate online

The above are just short search string examples. You can go a lot more in-depth and add more variations and modifiers. There are in-depth lesson on creating and using search strings in the Digiologist Digital Marketing course.

Also, a useful tip is to increase your search results per page from 10 to 100. This just gives you more results on one page and you don't waste time clicking next again and again. To do this, click on the settings wheel at the top right hand corner on a Google search results page and choose 'search settings'. Go to where it says 'results per page' and set to 100.

Steps Involved: Local SEO

Local SEO involves applying techniques to rank in local search results that provide relevant results to users based on their location. For example, if a user located in New York searches for the term 'ice cream shops' and gets ice cream shops located in the UK as results, it wouldn't be useful at all right? Local SEO makes sure users get results relevant to their location.

Local SEO practices are important for businesses that have a fixed physical location and get a significant chunk of their business form that particular location.

This allows you to be visible to local customers in local search results and appear on map results as well which is important because it shows your location and contact information and is visible to people looking for your business while they're out and about. This contact information appears in the search results so people don't need to open your website and specially look for your contact information.

Local SEO involves making efforts in the following areas:

1. Google My Business Page
2. On site on-page optimization with geo-targeted keywords
3. Citation Building
4. Reviews
5. Local Links (local sites, local directories)

Google My Business Page:

The Google My Business page is the main Google

account you need to set up for local SEO currently but local SEO has been changing frequently over the past couple of years so expect more changes soon. The main profile to be created was called Google Places in 2011. It was called Google + Local in 2012 and currently it is called Google My Business, which you can sign up for at google.com/business.

Setting up your Google My Business page is quite easy. Just follow the steps at google.com/business. It instructs you on adding all of your information such as business name, categories, address, phone number, operating hours etc. You get to add pictures, link to your website and add a description. In case your business has multiple locations, you can add their info in bulk by importing a file.

Tips for setting up your Google business page:

1. Have as many images as possible and make sure they're high resolution. In addition to general photos, add a good profile and cover photo as well.
2. Add a keyword rich description.
3. Choose the your business categories with care.
4. Add a local phone number with the local code over a toll free number.

There could be a chance that your listing might have already been created before so you don't need to make a new one. In that case you need to claim the existing one and make any changes if necessary. When you start filling in your details, Google will let you know if you need to make a new one or claim an already existing one. Your profile also needs to be verified. This is done by entering a code Google will mail to your business address in a few weeks to verify that your location is real.

On-Site Optimization:

Add your NAP to every page of your site in the footer. If you're unsure on how to format your NAP, see the citation building section below. Target geo-targeted keywords on your site as well. These are keywords you normally target as well but with a location modifier added. Add them to your page titles, meta descriptions, page content etc like you normally do on-page SEO, except that in this case, you're inserting geo-targeted keywords into your site pages.

Also make a page on your site for each location in case of multi-location businesses and have your URL structures that reflect that. For e.g., if your business has locations in New York, Los Angeles and Chicago, set your pages to:

www.example.com/locations/new-york
www.example.com/locations/los-angeles
www.example.com/locations/chicago

Citation Building:

Citations are a very important part of local seo and are similar to links and involve citation building, similar to link building. A citation is an online reference to your business NAP on external sites. NAP is an acronym for name, address and phone number and that's exactly what a citation is, your business name, address and phone number combination. Citation building is similar to link building except that citations don't link to your site, as in they're not clickable hyperlinked links but rather just a collection of text in the NAP format.

The way it is similar to link building is that is involves the process of building as many citations on external sites as possible. Build profiles on local directories and add your citations there and also in the footer on every page on your site.

Here is a commonly used format for citations:

Company Name,
Company Address,
City,
State/Province,
Postal Code/Zip Code
Phone Number

The above format can be changed around as well, as long as they make sense and are in the right order. For example, you can have the city and state/province in one line together as well or have the city, state/province as well as zip/postal code all in one line. As long as it is a NAP combination in the right order.

Here's an example on how an actual citation would look like:

ABC Solutions,
72 Highland Ridge,
Midvale,
Utah,
84073
(801)3467-9652

*Note that the above information is a false address and number for demonstration purposes only.

Putting your NAP together is quite easy but complications arise when there is no NAP consistency in citation building. The way you initially decide to format your NAP is exactly how each citation needs to be built. Inconsistency will occur even in small cases such as addition of or removal of a space, addition of a dot or just general changing of the format.

You can find citation opportunities through manual searches as well as by using the Whitespark Citation Finder tool (whitespark.ca/local-citation-finder). You can also track your local rankings for different location based keywords using any of he following: Georanker (georanker.com), Whitespark Local Rank Tracker (whitespark.ca/local-rank-tracker) and Brightlocal

(brightlocal.com/seo-tools).

You can also track where your competitors are getting their citations from, just like you can check their backlinks in the case of link building. Track your competitors citation courses using the above mentioned tools. To get a bit of an idea where your competitors citations are coming from, you can also do a manual search without any tools. To do that, just Google the competitor's name and zip/postal code together and you'll get results of all of the pages with their citations. You can also add the subtraction modifier as: -competitorsite.com to eliminate results of all of the pages with citations from the competitors site.

Google+ Reviews:

Getting favourable reviews and a good star rating is important for local SEO as a ranking factor and also a conversion factor. Good reviews and ratings influence people to make purchases. The best people to ask for reviews are your customers ofcourse. These are people that have already tried out your product/service and are eligible to give their thoughts on it.

A lot of companies incentivize their customers for leaving them reviews by offering them a free product or discount on their next purchase. This is against Google's terms though. It's better to be safe in this case instead of being penalized. There is no restriction against asking for reviews though so ask your customers to leave you reviews. Do this as a soft sell though so don't pressurize them. You can ask them verbally and also print it on your corporate packaging so they're reminded later on.

It also helps significantly if you ask for reviews on your website and add a quick tutorial video or written list of steps on how to leave a review. As surprising as it may sound, some people are confused on how to do it. Ofcourse another obvious way to get reviews, and good reviews that is, is to be so good that your customers love your product and want to review you.

Local Links:

Build as many links and citations on local sites as possible. These are sites in your city like city specific blogs and news sites and directories. Find these sites manually using search strings by adding local modifiers and citation finder tools like White Spark.

When Things Go Wrong: Penalties and Algorithmic Changes

Search engines change their algorithms i.e. ranking factors from time to time to improve their results and prevent irrelevant lower quality websites from ranking.

When a new algorithm change takes place, your website could get hit and lose all its rankings, thus lowering traffic significantly. However, a point to note here is that the algorithms only affect sites taking part in more black hat spammy practices. These are known as search engine penalties.

White Hat vs Black Hat SEO:

White hat SEO contains all of the SEO practices that are in compliance with search engine regulations. These practices are non spammy and aim to prove value to site owners and include ranking techniques that are fair and clean. Black hat on the other hand involves practices that are not in compliance with search engine regulations and involve manipulation and deception to rank.

An example of doing the same work through white hat and black hat methods can be explained in the case of link building. A white hat approach to building links would be through publishing good quality content that earns links over time. A black hat approach would be purchasing links instead on sites across the web. Black hat methods don't have long lasting effects and are ultimately caught by search engines and the sites are penalized. Some other examples of black hat SEO include using keywords numerous times in articles just for ranking purposes i.e. keyword stuffing, comment spamming, aggressive profile creation using softwares, using hidden invisible text to stuff keywords etc.

Past Algorithm Changes:

Search engine algorithmic changes take place all the time. Some of the popular ones that affected people the most have been Panda, Penguin and Hummingbird. The first version of the panda update took place in February 2011 and de-ranked all sites with poor quality content. Hummingbird was released in September 2013 and aimed to provide better search results keeping in mind the context of the search. This update was not meant to penalize sites but to provide better and more accurate results matching the intention of the users query.

Avoiding Penalties:

Read into Google's 'Webmaster Guidelines' and follow them to prevent being hit by a penalty. The guidelines consist of basic rules such as avoiding writing low quality content, avoiding publishing duplicate content, no thin content, no keyword stuffing and more. View the webmaster guidelines document for more details at support.google.com/webmasters

How to Know You've Been Hit by a Penalty:

Two types of penalties can hit you: manual penalties, algorithmic penalties.

If you're hit by a manual penalty by Google's team, you'll get a message in your Google Webmasters account stating that. Manual penalties are ones in which a member of Google's webspam prevention department finds you breaking any of the Webmaster Guidelines and manually reports you in the system. You'll know if you've been hit by a manual penalty if you get a message in your Google Webmasters account.

Algorithmic penalties on the other hand, affect all websites and happen when Google updates the way websites are ranked i.e. updates an algorithm. You'll know if you've been hit by a penalty if you experience a drop in traffic and rankings. It's a good idea to keep a check on your ranking positions using tools like Rank Tracker (moz.com/tools/rank-tracker) and Positionly (positionly.com).

What to Do If You've Been Hit By a Penalty:

Either of disavows or reconsiderations are the answer based on what you've been penalized for. You can disavow your backlinks that you believe are not good quality and harming your sites ranking abilities. Disavowing links does not remove the links but it tells Google to not consider them when assessing your site. A reconsideration request requests Google to look into your site after you've made actions to fix the problems stated in the manual action notification in Google Webmasters.

Disavow Process:

Disavow links using the Google Disavow tool, which you can find at: google.com/webmasters/tools/disavow-links-main.
You need to first download all of your links, then choose the ones you want disavowed and then upload a list of just the ones you want disavowed. This document needs to be in .txt form and should be uploaded in the search console of your webmasters area. The list of links to be disavowed needs to be presented following a specific format which looks like: domain:example.com. The list of links you have that you want to disavow will most probably have sites following different formats such as http:// or www. To remove all of those http and www's in bulk use a disavow generator (disavowgenerator.com) to save time.

Reconsideration Process:

Like mentioned above, reconsideration requests are only for manual penalties, a notification for which you receive in your Webmaster Tools account. Before you submit a reconsideration request, make sure you've made the changes required and fixed the issue the manual penalty was about.

When you're ready to submit the request, open your Webmaster Tools account and in the left hand sidebar click 'manual actions' under 'search traffic'. Click on 'request a review' and upload your reconsideration request document. This document needs to be in .txt version and should be written in a format similar to an email or letter and contain information on the work carried out to fix the problem.

Start the document with an introduction on what the penalty was for and very briefly explain what has been done to fix it. Then talk in more detail about the efforts made to fix the problem and provide proof as well. The proof can be supplied by providing information in a Google document or sheet in Google Drive and linking to it. Make sure your sheet access is set to public though so they can view it. This sheet can contain lists of links that have been removed or pages on your site that have been fixed etc. Give all of the information required in the proof sheet but keep the reconsideration document short. Remember that a real human from the Google webspam team will be reading this and it won't be computer read so don't make it too long. Also let them know what you'll be doing in the future and how you will make sure not to repeat the mistake again. A few things you should not do are: making it seem like it is Google's fault, anything abusive or going on and on about how the penalty has affected you and begging for forgiveness.

Tools and Helpful Sites

Helpful sites:

Dedupe List: Removes duplicates from lists of sites. This saves a lot of time when you've prospected sites to build links on and need to remove sites you may have entered more than once and don't want to spend hours removing them manually. Check it out at dedupelist.com.

URL Trimmer: Ever wanted to sort a list of sites alphabetically but can't because they're all in different formats such as www. or http://? You can use the SEO Weather URL trimmer to enter a list of sites and convert them to the same format so you can alphabetically order them. I have saved a lot of time with this neat little tool. Check it out at: seoweather.com/trim-urls-to-root-domain-standardise-urls-prefixes.

Bulk Link Opener: If you have a list of sites you want to open at once to examine, don't waste time clicking on them individually. Use the Ontolo Link Reviewer to open them all at once. Check it out at ontolo.com/link-building-url-reviewer.

Helpful Tools:

There are hundreds of SEO tools out there. The ones below are the most popular ones. Some of them are paid, some free. Most of the paid ones have trial versions you can try out before committing.

Site Structure:

Sitemap Generator: xml-sitemaps.com

Redirect Plugin: wordpress.org/plugins/redirection

Keyword Research:

Google Keyword Planner: adwords.google.ca/KeywordPlanner

Keyword Idea Tools: ubersuggest.org, keywordtool.io, wordtracker.com.

On-Page SEO:

Yoast SEO: Wordpress SEO plugin (wordpress.org/plugins/wordpress-seo)

Screaming Frog: Powerful tool that lets you check your pages with missing page titles, meta descriptions, duplicate titles and more (screamingfrog.co.uk/seo-spider/#download).

Link Building and Analysis:

Backlink checkers: Ahrefs (ahrefs.com), SEMrush (semrush.com).

Link Research Tools: Powerful tool that lets you

compare your competitor's links together and mine out their common backlinks, check your harmful backlinks, find your competitors strongest links, find your competitors link building rates, the anchor text usage ratios of your and your competitors backlinks and more. Check it out at linkresearchtools.com.

Link Prospector: Helps you find link building prospects to reach out to. It gives you a list of sites to get links on such as sites to guest post on, resource pages to get links from, reviews sites, donation sites and more, all based on your industry. Get it at linkprospector.citationlabs.com.

Check My Links: Check My Links is an extension that is a broken link finder. It highlights broken links on a page.

Site Metric Checkers: URL Profiler (urlprofiler.com) and Netpeak Checker (netpeak.net/software/netpeak-checker) are two site metric checkers that check DA, PA, PR and more in bulk.

Outreach:

Yesware: Lets you know which emails that you sent have been opened. Get it at yesware.com.

Yet Another Mail Merge: Lets you send customized emails (based on a template) in bulk using Google sheets. Get it at chrome.google.com/webstore/detail/yet-another-mail-merge/mgmgmhkohaenhokbdnlpcljckbhpbmef?hl=en.

Buzzstream: Tool for storing and sorting outreach databases, keeping a check on relationship stages with prospects, finding contact information and conducting outreach.

Raven Tools: A tool for storing links built to keep a database. It also keeps a check on which links you built have been removed and notifies you in such cases so you don't have to waste time checking links built.

Local SEO:

All three of the tools below perform some or all of the following: finding where to build citations, citation building, finding competitors citation sources, tracking local rankings and more. Since they perform similar functions, play around with them and see which one you like best:

Whitespark: whitespark.ca
Bright Local: brightlocal.com
Georanker: georanker.com

Miscellaneous:

Google Analytics: Provides you with a wealth of information your site performance through number of visitors to your site, how long they stayed on your site, which pages they landed on and exited from, how many were first time visitors and a lot more. Sign up at google.com/analytics.

Google Webmaster Tools: Gives you data to make sure your site is healthy and following guidelines. It notifies you in case there are any errors or site issues. Sign up at google.com/webmasters.

Rank Trackers: Moz Rank Tracker (moz.com/tools/rank-tracker), Positionly (positionly.com). They let you know which position your sites ranks at for the keywords you input and track your rank for you so you don't have to manually search your rank by searching your keyword and finding your site.

SEO FAQs

Do I need SEO?

A high ranking in search results are seen by hundreds of thousands of people and is important in bringing in traffic and leads which are both important for every business. So yes, you do need SEO. The higher you rank in search engines, the more clicks you get to your site and the more traffic you end up getting which ultimately leads to more sales.

Should I hire someone or do it myself?

SEO can get intimidating at times and whether you can do it yourself or not depends on your learning curve, your competition, your situation and how much time you can spend on it. It is mostly the larger companies that hire SEOs to do everything for them. If you are a small business it might not be in your budget. It is not impossible though. Through application of strategies, measuring results and making changes based on them, over time you should be able to learn it all and have your site rank higher. The basics are pretty simple but in case of problems such as penalties, things can get complicated. In the case of a penalty, seek professional help.

How long will it take to rank?

SEO efforts can take time to kick in. It all depends on who is outranking you and how strong their site is. For certain keywords, the sites outranking you will be a lot more powerful and so ranking for those keywords can take months, maybe even up to a year to rank well for. On the other hand, less competitive keywords can take a few days to a few weeks worth of efforts. To get an idea of how competitive your main keywords are, see who ranks for them and check their site metrics and backlinks and compare them all to your site and see how your site fares against them.

How is SEO different from SEM?

SEO involves making efforts to rank in search engines organically whereas SEM involves paid efforts such as PPC in addition to ranking organically. In short, SEM is SEO + PPC.

How do search engines work and rank?

Search engines use robots (also popularly called spiders) to crawl websites and make note of their content while scanning them. This is all done extremely fast and needs to be done fast since there are so many sites to go through. Based on the content the robots find on sites and a variety of other factors the sites are ranked based on relevancy and usefulness.

How does Google find my website?

There are many ways Google can find your website. When you launch your site for the first time, a good practice is to manually submit your site URL to search engines. You can submit your site here: google.com/webmasters/tools/submit-url. Creating a sitemap also helps Google in finding deeper pages on your site. The backlinks you get from other sites also help in your pages being discovered and crawled faster.

Why isn't my website showing up on Google?

If you have a new website, most probably the reason why it's not showing up on Google is because the search robots haven't crawled it yet. On an average it takes around 10 days for Google to crawl a new website or even an existing one with fresh changes made. To speed up the process, manually submit your site to Google in Webmaster Tools. For sites that have been up for a while, it is unlikely to not show up in search results. A possibility could be that the site is ranking many pages behind in the results that it is impossible to find the rank number manually. In that case, fill your site and a few keywords into rank tracking tools (see links for them in the tools page) and they will tell you which page your site is on. At times your site could be hundreds of pages into the search results which makes it impossible to find your site manually. This doesn't mean your site isn't on Google. It's just far behind in the results.

Why is my website no longer on Google?

You might have completely lost rankings due to a

penalty or could have a drop in rankings. Remember that a drop in rankings is different from being completely removed from the results. Enter your site and the keywords you're no longer ranking for in rank checker tools such as Positionly and Rank Tracker and check whether you no longer rank for the keyword or rank very late in the rankings. If you no longer rank for them, check your Google Analytics account and see if you have had a sharp drop in traffic and check your Google Webmaster Tools account for any notifications or messages regarding a penalty. You've most likely been hit by a penalty. If you're still ranking but have been moved further down, it's most likely because you either had a low click through rate, high bounce rate or other sites suddenly seemed more relevant for the term than you either because of their on-page optimization or increase in backlinks.

What is the difference between crawling and indexed?

The simplest way to put it is that crawling is the process of finding information and indexing is the process of storing information. Search engines efforts can be explained in three broad steps: crawling, indexing and retrieving. During crawling, search engine robots visit pages and analyze their content, during indexing, the information regarding certain words and content and their location is saved and during retrieving, the Google algorithms look up the search terms in the index and provide relevant results.

Part 3: Pay Per Click

Introduction to Pay Per Click

Pay Per Click Marketing:

Pay per click marketing, commonly referred to as 'PPC', is a means of advertising on search engines in which advertisers pay when their ads are clicked. These ads appear above the organic search results.

PPC is sort of like buying your way into ranking in search engines rather than earning your way in. It can takes months to rank in the organic part of the search results but pay per click allows you to rank in the paid section in a matter of days and at times, hours. Pay per click marketing is based on a bidding model where advertisers place bids on keywords they'd like to appear for in searches for them. For more competitive keywords, your bids should to be higher to be accepted and show up in searches for them. Google shows your ad based on a variety of factors such as your bid compared to others, your quality score etc.

Landing Pages:

After they click on your ad, visitors land on your site, more specifically a page on your site called the landing page. This landing page is 11very important because the design and layout decides whether the person that clicks on your ad will convert to a sale or not. The landing page needs to be captivating enough to keep the visitor on your page and not leave without reading the content of the page and ultimately, clicking on the CTA i.e. call to action. The biggest mistake most people make while creating PPC campaigns is, they lead the PPC ad to the site's home page. This just confuses the person that clicks the ad and makes them search for what they were looking for when they clicked the ad. Make the landing page relevant to the ad so your visitors don't have to search for anything. You could lead the ads to your home page though, in case your home page is set up landing page style and represents what the ad is about. If the ad advertises a book, link the ad to a landing page about the book with a 'buy' or 'purchase' CTA. Make this entire process as simple as possible for the visitor. Effective landing pages can result in higher conversion rates i.e. more leads and can reduce bounce rate, thus increasing your Google quality score.

Conversion Rate Optimization:

Conversion rate optimization is the process of increasing the rate of lead generation. It involves increasing the amount of visitors to your site that convert to customers. Not everyone who visits your site will purchase from you. CRO involves increasing the percentage of visitors that turn into customers. It involves split testing changes to elements of your landing pages to see what works in creating the most conversions from a visitor to your site to an actual sale. CRO is mostly implemented with the aim of increasing sales but at times it can be for other actions as well (that all ultimately are sales related) such as having visitors download an eBook or whitepaper or having them sign up for your newsletter etc. A conversion simply refers to having the visitors to your site complete an action that you want them to take.

Steps Involved: PPC

PPC steps explained briefly:

1. Decide the content of your ad, your goal and your landing page.
2. Sign up for an AdWords account at google.com/adwords
3. Search for and choose the keywords you want your ad to show up for. You can choose these keywords based on their traffic and competitiveness using the Google Keyword Planner.
4. Create an ad with a compelling title, description and a link to the page you want people to land on.
5. Add your billing information and daily spending limits so your ad is stopped being displayed once it reaches your daily budget in click costs (or impression costs if you opt for that).
6. Launch the ad and see how it performs. Based on the results make any changes required such as removing low performing keywords, changing ad copy etc.

Deciding Ad Content, Goals, Landing Pages:

Decide what your ad is going to be for, what your goal is and your landing page design. Decide which networks you want your ad shown to and which format you want to go with.

Ads are mainly shown to two networks and in two formats:

1. Search Network: These are the text ads that appear in text form on the search engine results pages above the organic search results.

2. Content Network: These ads are in image form i.e. display ads and are shown across websites that have AdSense enabled.

If you plan on advertising on both networks, it is advised to choose keywords separately for both and create separate accounts. This just allows for two separate campaigns and more clarity.

Some of the different goals for your PPC campaign can be to increase traffic, increase brand awareness, increase sales. Based on what your goal is, choose the network you want your ad to be shown to, your landing page destination, landing page design and call to action. For example, if your aim is to increase traffic, you're mainly going to be concerned with the click through rate from your ad to your site and if your aim is to increase sales, you're going to be concerned with conversion rate. Once you've decided your ad content, ad purpose and have your landing page set up, you're ready to create your ad.

Keyword Research:

Keyword research for PPC is similar to keyword research for on-page SEO. It's a good idea to brainstorm a list of keywords yourself first without a tool and build off that using tools. Refer to the section on keyword research in the SEO section of this book.

The main tool you need to use for keyword research is the Google Keyword Planner, available at: adwords.google.com/KeywordPlanner. You may need to fully sign up for AdWords before you access the tool.

In the first option, 'search for new keywords', there will be a box to enter your product or service. Enter that information. Then choose your category from the drop down menu. Then choose your target language and country in the demographics section. You can also add a specific city if you're not targeting the whole country. You can also select a very specific region as well (click on 'advanced search' for that). Adding your target location will make sure that the data you get back for your chosen keywords is only for your target area so you know how many people are searching for those terms in the locations your ad will be shown. You can add keyword filters as well to set a number on the highest or lowest search traffic your targeted keywords should have and their competition. This is very helpful in finding keywords that have combinations of good search traffic and low to medium competition i.e. keywords that are easier to show up for. It's a good idea to set a low number first and play around with it all and build your quality score. If it goes well you can always add more keywords later with higher search traffic. Giving a standard number of the average search traffic for keywords you should go for is difficult because it greatly depends on your industry but an approximate number of around 5k-10k searches a month should be good to start off with. Also choose whether you want the data for keyword performance for only Google ads or on Google partner sites such as AOL, YouTube etc as well. Once you've filled in all of the information, click 'get ideas'.

It will then give you a list of keyword ideas based on your category and product. You have two options to view this data: ad group ideas or keyword ideas. The keyword ideas tab shows data for individual keywords and the ad group ideas tab shows data for a group of keywords that are very similar. Based on the average monthly searches and competition, choose all of the keywords you want to appear for by clicking the arrow that appears under 'add to plan'.

Choose as many keywords as you can and see how they perform. Let a keyword run for atleast one mille (1000 impressions) before you decide whether to keep it or not and keep the ones with a good quality score. You can have up to 2000 keywords per ad group, 100 ad groups per campaign and 25 campaigns per account.

You can also add negative keywords to prevent your ad being displayed to irrelevant searches. For eg. Suppose you're a lawyer and you don't provide free consultations and even your initial consultations are paid. You'd want to add 'free legal advice' to your negative keywords as this is something a lot of people search for and you don't want to show up for it and waste your budget. Then download your keyword list and move on to ad creation.

Steps for Ad Creation:

Steps for setting up your ad:

1. Set up an account at google.com/adwords. Fill in the introductory information required such as your name, company name, email, billing details etc.
2. Choose between the options of only search network, only display network or both networks.
3. Enter your keywords. Upload them altogether as the document you downloaded during the keyword research stage to save time.
4. Set your bid and choose your daily budget. It will then give you a rough idea of how many impressions and clicks you'll get based on that information so you can increase or decrease

your bid and budget based on that. You can also set your bid to manual or automatic. It is recommended you stick to manual and play around with your bid. Automatic bidding can cause problems and lead to very high bids. It will give you a suggested bid as well, which is good to get an idea of what your bid should be around. Also remember that the higher you place your bid, the more the chances that your ad will show up. You only pay when people click on the ad, hence the term, pay per click. For all the times your ad is shown but no one clicks on it, you're not charged, unless you opt for a CPM model.

5. Write your ad content. Provide a landing page link, display link, ad headline and ad text. The display link is the one shown in the ad and is there to make the ad appear neater because your actual landing page link can have a long URL that can look quite messy. Your display link should be your homepage link. It will then give you a display of how your ad will look. Remember that the display link is different from the actual link that the searcher lands on after clicking the ad. While writing the ad, choose a compelling title and descriptive and interesting text so more people end up clicking on it.

6. Enter your billing information and save. It will then give you a summary of all the information. Review it and click 'create ad'. Your ad will then undergo the approval process before going live which is usually one business day.

Doing the above will create your AdWords account. Now when you open google.com/adwords, it will take you to your new AdWords dashboard. This dashboard will give you important information on how much budget has been utilized, impressions your ad has received, clicks your ad has received, how individual keywords are performing and more. You won't get any data till your ad has gone live and has been up for a few days so wait for that to happen. Also keep in mind that AdWords reporting is not real time. Data for most metrics is shown about 3 hours later.

Another important part of AdWords is quality score. Sometimes your competitors can bid less but have their ads shown more and rank higher. This is probably because their quality score is higher. Quality score is a score from 1 to 10 that judges the relevancy and usefulness of your ad for specific keywords. This score is given on a per keyword basis and is based on ad click through rate, relevancy of the keyword to the ad, relevancy of the landing page, quality of the landing page, landing page load time and your account history.

All of the above steps have been explained for PPC through Google AdWords. When people hear the term PPC, they immediately think about advertising on Google. However, PPC can take place on other sites as well such as Facebook, YouTube, Pinterest, Instagram, LinkedIn. Facebook and YouTube have their own PPC ad set up tools. Have you ever noticed those ads in the sidebar of your home feed when logged into your Facebook account or those ads that play before your YouTube video and the little banners that appear at the bottom of your video? That's all PPC. The steps for YouTube and Facebook advertising are a little different from setting up AdWords ads but the overall idea is the same.

Ad Campaign Upkeep:

The work doesn't end after creating the ad. There is a lot of upkeep when it comes to PPC campaigns. You need to monitor your spend daily, check which keywords are performing well and which aren't and more:

1. Check your spend daily and see how many impressions you're getting for your current budget and whether it is enough or your budget needs to be increased.
2. Adjust bids if you're not showing up for some keywords or if you want to improve your position.
3. Remove low performing keywords that you're not getting a good click through rate for.
4. Check which regions you're not performing too well in and remove ad targeting for them.
5. Test landing page content and design through split testing and remove the ones with lower conversion rates.

Landing Pages:

The web page that the users end up on after clicking your ad is the landing page. Your landing pages are very important for sales and if done right can increase the conversion rate significantly.

Create a good landing page experience by having your landing page contain information useful and relevant to the ad content, be engaging enough for the visitor to spend time on it and not click out and load fast.

Characteristics of a good landing page design:

1. A good compelling main heading. Try making this heading as relevant to the user as possible so it doesn't confuse the visitor.
2. A supporting headline
3. Information of the product/service and the offer that compels the visitor to convert
4. A photo. Make this a professional, inviting photo clearly portraying what you're offering so there is no confusion or guesswork involved.
5. A form to fill if required
6. A clear CTA for your conversion goal

The layout and design of your landing page is very important. Since there is no cookie cutter solution to landing pages as needs for different businesses are different, try looking up landing page examples for your industry for inspiration and ideas. Also snoop around your competitors sites and see what their landing pages look like. It is a good idea to split test a few landing pages as well and see which ones works best. If you have an in-house designer you can have them design your landing page. Else easily create one yourself using a landing page builder like Unbounce (unbounce.com), Lander (landerapp.com) or Lead Pages (leadpages.net).

Conversion Rate Optimization:

Conversion rate optimization is concerned with increasing the percent of visitors that convert by taking the action you want them to take. The action is mostly that of them becoming a customer and leading to a sale but at times it could also be wanting them to download a whitepaper, sign up for your newsletter etc. Improvements to your landing page design to increase CRO are all done based on analytics on metrics such as time on site, bounce rate, exit rate etc.

CRO is important because there is always room for improvement and having a visitor come to your site and not convert is a lost opportunity so you need to make all of the necessary changes and efforts to have as many visitors as possible convert into a sale. CRO is beneficial because it is only based on your efforts so it is free and it can significantly reduce your customer acquisition cost.

Helpful PPC Sites and Tools:

Helpful Sites:

Google AdWords: google.com/adwords

Google Keyword Planner: adwords.google.ca/KeywordPlanner

Instagram Advertising: business.instagram.com/advertising

Pinterest Advertising: ads.pinterest.com

Twitter Advertising: ads.twitter.com

Facebook Advertising: facebook.com/business

YouTube Advertising: youtube.com/yt/advertise

Yahoo Advertising: advertising.yahoo.com

Bing Advertising: bingads.microsoft.com

Helpful Tools:

Spyfu: Spyfu allows you to get access to your competitor's ad copy, keywords and bids. Check it out at: spyfu.com.

Negative Keyword Finder Tool: This tool is very easy to use and finds negative keywords based on your main keywords. Check it out at: wordstream.com/negative-keywords.

AdWords Editor: Powerful tool that saves you time by letting you make ad edits in bulk. Check it out at: google.com/intl/en_US/adwordseditor.

A/B Testing Software's: Easily split test landing pages using Optimizely (optimizely.com), VWO (vwo.com), Convert (convert.com).

Landing Page Developers: These sites help you easily create landing pages without a designer: Unbounce (unbounce.com), Lander (landerapp.com), Instapage (instapage.com), Lead Pages (leadpages.net).

PPC FAQs:

Why isn't my ad showing up on Google?

If your daily budget is set too low, either Google is showing your ad sparingly or your daily spend has been finished. Another reason could be that your ad is performing better in locations other than the one you're located in so Google is showing your ad in those locations only instead so you may never see your ad yourself simply because it's not being shown where you're searching from.

What is remarketing?

Remarketing helps you place your ad in front of people that have visited your site but not purchased your product. It allows you to follow the path of past website visitors and place ads on sites they're viewing.

How much should I bid and what should I set my budget to?

Your bids should be set on a per keyword basis and are something you need to play around with till you're happy with your ad ranks. Your budget also needs to be decided keeping in mind your product cost. You don't want to bid so high that your PPC campaign runs you in losses. Keep in mind that not everyone who clicks on your ad will convert, but you will end up paying for all clicks, even the ones that don't result in a sale. Your budget depends on your resources and also the number of impressions you want.

Why do search ads get more clicks than display ads?

The average CTR of search ads is around 2% and the average CTR for banner ads is 0.1-0.2% only. Search ads get a lot more clicks than display ads. The reason for that is that search ads are a lot more targeted as you have the options of having them shown to a very specific group of people based on their interests, demographics, regions which allows you to control where your ads appear and focus on audiences that are more likely to be interested in what you're selling.

What is a good conversion rate?

This depends on industry to industry. Fire Click has a very interesting publicly available benchmark index for various industries available at index.fireclick.com. Check out what your industry stats look like.

Part 4: Email Marketing

Introduction: Email Marketing

Email marketing is a method of direct digital marketing that uses email as the medium of conveying the commercial promotional message. Every email sent to a potential customer is considered email marketing. Email marketing works well because you get to send your message to your customers instead of having them come to read your message like in the case of websites.

Email marketing is mostly done by sending newsletters and other promotional emails to email lists businesses build over time. These email lists are built from user submitted emails that can be obtained from visitors by giving them something in return. A few examples of when they give their info is while signing up for the site newsletter or while filling a form before downloading something. The email is in most cases given in exchange for some incentive such as an eBook or a whitepaper.

Another method some marketers use, which is not recommended is non-permission based email marketing i.e. sending commercial emails to lists that are bought, rented or self built. Commercial emails that are sent to people who have not given their email themself are considered non-permission emails and have higher chances of being marked as spam. Another way of email marketing is to have your message placed in other businesses newsletters. This is a paid placement ofcourse.

Though you may feel that email doesn't sound as exciting as other mediums of marketing such as social media do, it is an effective marketing channel for many businesses. Email marketing was the first true method of communicating on the internet, before there were any social media sites. It may have started out as a method of personal communication but it grew as a tool for business communication as well.

The industry standard for email open rate is around 12%. That's more than the click rate most PPC ads get. Many say that email is dead. They either haven't tried it or didn't do it properly. It is most certainly not dead. Almost everyone uses email. Do you know anyone who doesn't have an email account? There are over 3 billion email accounts in the world. That's more that the users of most social media sites!

Steps Involved

There are three main methods of email marketing:

1. Advertising
2. Non-permission based
3. Permission based

The advertising method above refers to having your message placed in other businesses newsletters. This would involve getting in touch with businesses that aren't competitors but are in your industry (think adjacent markets) that have email lists built of people that are your potential customers as well and purchase ad space in their newsletter and get your message inserted in their next email send out.

The non-permission based email refers to sending bulk emails to email lists that are bought or rented or even self built. The people on these lists have not signed up and given you their email themselves and so haven't given you their permission to send them promotional emails. Do not buy or rent email lists. There are high chances that your email will get marked as spam and all future emails you send to everyone will end up going to their spam boxes.

The permission based email marketing is the method you should adopt. It complies with the CAN-SPAM Act (en.wikipedia.org/wiki/CAN-SPAM_Act_of_2003) that is against the sending out of unsolicited commercial emails. Permission based email marketing involves sending commercial emails or even regular newsletters to an email list that you've gathered from emails people gave themselves on your site and opted in to receiving emails. These emails are given when there is an incentive to join your email list like giving away something free and valuable such as a whitepaper, eBook, market study etc. Your email list subscribers are similar to Facebook likes, Twitter followers, YouTube subscribers etc. They need an incentive to subscribe and stay subscribed.

Ways to grow your email list:

1. Provide something valuable as an incentive for

providing their email. The thing of value is provided in exchange for their email and delivered after they give their email. Some examples of things you can provide are a whitepaper, market study, daily tips, product discount, tool, checklist, cheat sheet, video.

2. Take their email during registration when they purchase.
3. Host online events like webinars and take their email during sign up.
4. Record attendee's emails during offline events you're hosting or have set up a booth at.
5. Have multiple CTAs (call to actions) on your site. You can place these in the navigation bar, above the navigation bar, in the sidebar, in the footer, in the content etc.

You can add CTA's with some cool plugins and tools that are very easy to set up. Use Icegram (icegram.com) and Hello Bar (hellobar.com) to insert a header bar (above the navigation bar), Pop Up Domination (popupdomination.com) for pop ups, Un Pop (getunpop.com) for pop ups that appear in places on your site that don't cover the content so it doesn't annoy your reader, Interrupt (appsumo.com/interrupt) for placing email forms at the top of your content which disappear once the reader scrolls down.

It's really all about providing value in exchange for emails and placing clear CTAs at the right spots on your site and make sure your sign up forms are easy to fill.

Email Content:

Besides capturing emails, you need to know what to put in your emails and how to send them off. You can use email delivery software's such as Mailchimp (mailchimp.com) and AWeber (aweber.com) to deliver your newsletters and use their templates to get your format together.

Here are some of the important elements emails you need to focus on while putting your content together:

1. Subject Line: This is one of the first things the receiver sees and it greatly impacts whether they open the email or not so make it interesting.
2. Sender Address and Name: This is also one of the first things the receiver sees. Try to send the email from an actual person's name and email instead of the company name and a generic email such as info@example.com. You can set this information to the staff member who heads the newsletter or the founder's name.
3. Opening Line: The first sentence of the email actually shows up right next to the subject line and is visible to the readers before they even open the email.
4. Email Body: The email body is where your main content will be. Try to keep it as short as possible as shorter emails are more read.
5. Offer/Info/Update: Not all newsletters will have

an offer or an update as some newsletters are sent just to maintain a flow of communication as your company won't have an offer to send out each day or week. But during the times you do have something to announce, add that to the body.

6. CTA: Add a clearly visible call to action or a few CTA's (but no more than 3 as emails don't have as much space as websites) for whatever action you want the receivers to take.
7. Email Signature

These are the main elements of an email. But there are other things you need to add so your email complies with the rules and regulations of sending commercial email such as a clear unsubscribe option and a physical address. Read more about them in the CAN-SPAM Act.

Don't send emails with one huge image and with text in the image. Sometimes images don't load and so your email will actually appear as a blank mail. So break up your email into text and email parts. In case your email receiver receives the email with images turned off, they won't see the images but they'll be able to see the alt text of the images so name your image file names with the description and descriptive alt text.

Do a lot of split testing. Split test everything – subject lines, email content, CTAs. Email sending software's such as Mailchimp have this built in so it's easier to split test and get the data right there in your dashboard.

Metrics to Analyze:

Your email analytics will be available to you in the dashboard of the email sending software you use. Out of all of that data, you need to focus on open rates, attrition rates and click through rates. Open rate, as the name suggests is the percentage of people that opened your email compared to the ones that received your email. The ones that did not receive your email such as in the case of closed down email accounts are not included in the calculation of open rate. Email attrition rate is the rate of people no longer receiving your email. This could be due to them unsubscribing or their emails closed down. Click through rate is the rate of people who click on the CTA in your email.

Here are the formulas of the above and some other email metrics to keep an eye on:

Open Rate = Emails Opened / Emails Delivered

Click Through Rate = Click Throughs / Emails Delivered

Attrition Rate = Number of People No Longer Receiving emails / total number of emails on your list

Conversion Rate = Number of Actions Taken / Emails

Delivered

Unsubscribe Rate = Unsubscribes / Emails Delivered

You can also calculate the adjusted formulas by replacing emails delivered with emails opened.

Helpful Email Marketing Tools and Sites

Helpful Sites:

CAN-SPAM Act: Governs the rules and regulations of commercial email sending. Check it out at: en.wikipedia.org/wiki/CAN-SPAM_Act_of_2003

Helpful Tools:

Email Marketing Software's: MailChimp (mailchimp.com), AWeber (aweber.com)

Email Lead Capture Plugins:

Icegram (icegram.com) and Hello Bar (hellobar.com) insert header bars (above the navigation bar), Pop Up Domination (popupdomination.com) for pop ups, Un Pop (getunpop.com) for pop ups that appear in places on your site that don't cover the content so it doesn't annoy your reader, Interrupt (appsumo.com/interrupt) for placing email forms at the top of your content which disappear once the reader scrolls down.

Email Marketing FAQs

How often should I send emails?

This could be once a month, once a week, once a day. It depends on a variety of factors such as how much content you have to share, what your message is. You don't want to send emails infrequently and be forgotten but you also don't want to bombard them. Once a week is what most marketers stick to. It's also a good idea to ask your recipients how frequently they want to be emailed. Based on that you can segment your list based on how often the want to be emailed and create separate emails for the lists.

What day and time is the best to send emails?

This all depends on who your audience is and what their behavior is like. It depends on a variety of factors such as if they're reading their email from work or home, if they've signed up for your emails from their work email or personal email, which time zone they live in etc. So look into the demographics of your audience for that. It also depends on what you're selling. If you have an ecommerce site, most people will be buying on paydays. Monitor your open and click through rates for a better idea as well. Usually lower open rates occur on Mondays and Fridays and they are the highest mid-week around lunchtime.

Can I send emails to an email list I bought? What about emails I find online?

Don't send commercial emails to lists that are bought, rented or even self made by collecting emails. This only applies to emails that are commercial. Sending emails to such lists is against the CAN-SPAM Act and is also not going to give much benefit because these people don't know you and haven't opted in so they are more likely to mark your email as spam or not even open it.

How do I prevent my emails from landing in the spam box?

Ask your recipients to add your email to their address book or trusted sender list. Update your SPF (sender policy framework) Network. Your SPF framework is a document that provides information on who is a verified sender of emails on your behalf and matches domain and IP addresses of them while sending emails. If they don't match, chances of your email reaching the spam folder are much higher. So add your email marketing software as a sender in it.

Part 5: Social Media Marketing

Introduction: Social Media Marketing

Social media marketing involves promoting your business on social media sites i.e. sites that enable users to create and share content and network with one another. Social media is different from most marketing platforms. Social media was traditionally not designed to be a marketing medium, but rather a platform for the everyday person to communicate and network. It slowly evolved into a marketing platform for business owners. Compared to other marketing platforms like radio, magazines etc, social media is the only platform where consumers themselves create content too and that makes it a very community like consumer centric platform which you can master and get so much out of if you understand your audience right.

Social media channels are an opportunity to expand your reach and create brand awareness. Suppose there was an event that millions of people were going to be attending and you were given the chance to speak at the event or set up a stall for free. You'd never miss that opportunity right? That's what social media represents. An online real time event taking place with millions of visitors and you have a chance to set up your stall, in this case your profile, for free. Social media if done right, is free advertising. You can't pass it up.

Below are some of the most popular social platforms:

1. Facebook

2. Twitter
3. Pinterest
4. Instagram
5. LinkedIn 1
6. YouTube
7. Google+

Note that not all of the above are sites. Though Instagram is available to log into in it's site format, it started off as an app and is primarily used in app form. YouTube has been mentioned above as well and is one of the sites most people often forget is a social media site. Granted it operates more search engine style, it is still a social platform where people create and share content, just in video form. Besides the platforms above, there are other popular social sites as well such as Reddit, Stumbleupon, Digg and Delicious which are social bookmarking sites and important as well.

Steps Involved: Social Media Marketing

There are various social media platforms you can use for your business. You don't have to use all of them though. You can give them all a try and see which ones work best for you. There are hundreds of social media platforms out there but the ones with the widest reach are going to be discussed:

1. Facebook
2. Twitter
3. LinkedIn
4. Pinterest
5. Instagram
6. Google+
7. YouTube

Read their descriptions below to get a sense of which ones are more appropriate for your business. They all require a slightly different approach and steps, even though the overall idea is the same. Publishing content and using social media platforms has become quite simple over the years so we're not going to be discussing how to set up profiles but to learn more about the steps of creating and using profiles and PPC advertising on social media platforms, check out the Digiologist video course. This book is going to cover more on the pro's, cons, nature of the platforms, who they're better suited for and special features.

Facebook:

An integral part of most people's online presence and the most popular social networking site. It started off as a site aiming to connect college students but is now a networking platform for everyone to stay in touch with old friends, colleagues, family. Facebook currently has over a billion users. It's mainly a casual and friendly site so keep your tone light and friendly.

Businesses can use Facebook by creating either or all of: groups, events, pages. Facebook pages are the most commonly used by businesses. They operate in a way similar to personal profiles. You can add photos, status updates, share content from your site, share other pages content and more. They're like public profiles. Groups are more community centric where people come together to discuss a common topic. You can create a group for your businesses if applicable to create a community around your product or service where customers can become members and interact with one another about your product. Events can be used to attract more people to attend your company events whether online or offline such as webinars, product launches etc.

You can create a page at facebook.com/pages/create. To create a group, while on your homepage, click on 'groups' in the left hand sidebar and then click on 'create group' in the top right hand corner. To create an event, go to your business page and click 'offer, event +' (it's at the top of the timeline) and select 'event'. Add your event details and click 'create'.

While creating your Facebook page, group or event, keep SEO in mind and use any relevant keywords. Facebook pages rank too so that's important. Also keep local seo in mind and add your operating hours. Link your website as well and provide a brief introduction to your company. When it comes to posting on your page, you have a variety of options such as posting images, status updates covering any company news or product launches, sharing a link to your latest blog post or even sharing other pages content. Remember to take advantage of the Facebook cover page option. It's something most people first look at. You can change your cover photo from time to time and use it to display information on any current promotions or other important news you want to promote. To make sure you get the sizing correct, you can easily and quickly create cover photos using Fotor (fotor.com/features/facebook.html).

To see what other people are doing and get inspired by companies really using Facebook well, check out Facebook Studio (facebook-studio.com). It showcases companies with stunning profiles and unique campaign ideas. As far as performance measurement goes, Facebook analytics is pretty great but if you want to dig deeper you can check out other data providers like Simply Measured (simplymeasured.com) or Unmetric (unmetric.com).

Twitter:

Twitter is a social platform specializing in micro-blogging. Posts shared, which are popularly known as tweets are short and limited to 140 characters. It currently has over 200 million active users. Because tweets are so short, you need to be able to describe what you want to say in a few sentences only because every word counts. You don't get an entire about me section to fill on Twitter. Just a short bio, which again, needs to be kept short (160 characters).

Hashtags are widely used on Twitter (see more on hashtags below) and are important because they expose your brand to a much wider audience. Use hashtags that are popular so your tweet can show up in searches for them. Limit hashtags to one per tweet though. Other than tweets, you can interact with fans directly by sending them direct messages (on an individual level). If your fans tweet you something positive you like, 'favourite' the tweet to show appreciation or re-tweet them. Also use URL shorteners like Bitly (bitly.com) or Google URL Shortener (goo.gl) to make your links considerably smaller to save characters since you're limited. One of the cool Twitter features is that you can use search strings and conduct advanced searches and find exactly what you're looking for.

To find out more about your Twitter followers and find more people to follow, check out Followerwonk

(followerwonk.com) and Twellow (twellow.com).

LinkedIn:

LinkedIn is the largest professional social network with over 200 million users. It connects current and past colleagues to each other and present, past and potential employers to employees. Besides having a personal LinkedIn profile for yourself and all of your employees and stating you currently work at your company, an individual company page is important. Make a company page and fill in all of the necessary information like number of employees, location, about section etc. LinkedIn company pages work similar to Facebook pages. You can share images, news about the company or new products or promotions, link to articles etc. However, the tone of your posts needs to be kept formal, unlike Facebook where you can get away with sharing more informal information such as photos of company outings. Another thing you can do is ask your customers for reviews. These reviews, called recommendations are posted to individual profiles and not company pages so the founder of the company or other higher authorities can ask for reviews from the customers to their profiles. This works best for the service industry over the product industry though. LinkedIn also has groups on various topics which are similar to Facebook groups where people with a common interest come forward to discuss the topic and ask and answer questions. You have the opportunity of joining a few groups for your industry and stepping in from time to time to answer questions. This highlights your profile in front of people looking for answers and can result in sales as you come off as an expert in the field. Blogging on LinkedIn is popular as well. You can write articles on hot topics in your industry that you think would be appreciated and shared. These articles are similar to the ones for your company blog, except that they're published and kept on LinkedIn.

Pinterest:

Pinterest, with over 100 million users, is one of the social networks where you can get a large amount of referral traffic to your site easily. A lot of people have the image of Pinterest being a place for only pinning wedding planning images, recipes, home decor ideas only but that is far from the truth. Because of that a lot of businesses don't even consider joining Pinterest! You can find anything and everything on Pinterest such as SEO infographics, legal advice to even plumbing how-to's. Search your industry on Pinterest and you'll be surprised to see all sorts of content there. Once you set up your profile, create boards and pin images to them. Think of boards as folders, so you create boards for separation in regards to topics or content type. For e.g. if you're a law firm practicing corporate and personal injury law, create separate boards for each. If you want to share a variety of content types and formats such as tips, how-to's, videos, infographics, create separate boards for them. Your boards are there to help you organize your content. Which images can you pin? You can pin the images you use on your site in your blog content, royalty free images with your own text regarding them, re-pin other pins on Pinterest to your own boards and pin images from other websites using their link. You can pin videos too.

SEO is important when it comes to Pinterest because it works similar to search engines. People search for pins for certain keywords and you want your pins to show up for those searches so provide relevant descriptions for your boards and pins. Also turn on your profile search visibility so your pins and boards can rank in search engine results too. Another important tip is to add a pinterest image pinner plugin (wordpress.org/plugins/jquery-pin-it-button-for-images) to your site so visitors to your site can pin your images. They'll be pinning your images to their boards, but the pins will still link back to your site as the source so you end up getting more exposure and backlinks.

Google Plus:

Google Plus, being a Google product is really important as it has a direct and powerful impact on search rankings. It is the only search engine in which posts pass link equity. Since it is Google's own platform and important for ranking, optimize your Google+ profile with keywords in your about section. It's also important for local seo rankings so create a Google My Business page. It operates in a way that is different from other platforms with features such as

+1s and circles. Google+ circles allows people to add others in their various circles. This feature allows you to view content posted by people you add as well as share content with relevant people by sharing only to specific circles. The +1 button is similar to the 'like' button on Facebook. Users +1 a post when they like it. The posts you +1 may be shown to those in your circles and the posts people in your circles +1 may show up on your home feed. All of this may or may not happen because not all posts that are +1'd are shown as an action. This is done to avoid cluttering the feed. The posts that are shown are the ones that are thought to be the most relevant to the person viewing them.

YouTube:

YouTube is the most popular video content sharing platform. With over 1 billion users, it reaches more people than cable television and after Google, YouTube is the second largest search engine. Because it functions as a search engine, optimizing your content is important. Not only should you optimize your videos, but also your channel and playlists because they rank in YouTube search results as well. Add your targeted keywords into your channel-wide tags and about section to optimize your channel. Add your keywords into your playlist names and playlist descriptions and add relevant videos to them to optimize your playlists. Add keywords to your video titles, video descriptions, video tags and transcriptions to optimize your videos.

YouTube creators profiles are known as 'channels' which is where the videos uploaded are displayed and people who want to keep up up with your videos who follow your channel are called subscribers. Activity and engagement is important on YouTube so try to reply to comments and follow a posting schedule so you put out content regularly for your viewers. How-to videos are extremely popular on YouTube so try creating more instructional videos for your industry. Since YouTube requires creating content and not just sharing links or images, it takes up a lot more time compared to other social platforms and because of that it falls under the category of content marketing in a way and has been explained more in the content marketing section.

Besides the above, there are other sites as well such as Tumblr, Quora, Reddit, Digg, Stumbleupon, Delicious. There are also various niche specific social media sites as well which you should look into for your industry. Though they're not as popular as the above, their users are very specific so they can bring in very targeted traffic.

Advertising:

Most of the above platforms have their own ad placement options which operate similar to Adwords, on a PPC or CPM basis. Tutorials for each are available in the Digiologist video course.

Facebook: facebook.com/business
Twitter: ads.twitter.com
LinkedIn: linkedin.com/advertising
Pinterest: ads.pinterest.com
Instagram: business.instagram.com/advertising
YouTube: youtube.com/yt/advertise

Examples of the kind of content to post:

1. Product launches
2. Ongoing promotions like discounts and other offers
3. Blog content
4. Adjacent content
5. Share posts from other sites
6. Any recent images, videos
7. Contests
8. Events
9. Respond to FAQs
10. Provide an opinion on a trending topic in your industry
11. Re-share content from other pages your audience might enjoy
12. Polls to get your audience's opinion on present or future products

Some tips and best practices:

1. Brand your social media profiles. Use your logo and company colours to customize and take advantage of cover photo options that some platforms have.

2. Don't spam. Posting too frequently will not get you any new followers but instead drive away the ones you already have. Go for quality over quantity. As far as choosing the frequency of posting goes, don't overdo it and test out to see what number of posts are well accepted by your audience.
3. Engage with your audience. It's not possible to reply back to every comment but try to reply back to as many as possible. You can have an assistant do this for you if it gets too
4. Use URL shorteners such as Bitly (bit.ly) while posting links to save space. Bit.ly is also useful because it gives you the total number of clicks your link got.
5. Don't only post commercial content.
6. Use scheduling tools such as Hootsuite to schedule content across your social platforms to save time.
7. Deal with negative feedback in a positive manner. Look into the problem and try to solve it instead of ignoring or deleting the comment.

Also add social sharing buttons all across your site as well as icons to your profiles. These are two different things: socially connecting vs socially sharing. The icons will link to your social media profiles which your site visitors can check out and follow. The social sharing buttons are for the individual pieces of content and pages on your site that your visitors can click to share on their social profiles. Social media isn't just about creating profiles, but also the shares you automatically get when people share you on their profiles. For that create share worthy content. Also remember that having the most number of likes on social media doesn't mean anything if it doesn't result in leads. So don't go by numbers. They are important to track but not everything. The quality and value of your audience matters more.

Helpful Social Media Marketing Sites and Tools:

Social sharing buttons for Wordpress: en-ca.wordpress.org/plugins/social-media-feather

Social media profile icons for Wordpress: wordpress.org/plugins/ultimate-social-media-icons

Hashtagify: Gives you ideas for popular hashtags being used in your industry and their usage volumes. Check it out at hashtagify.me.

Hootsuite: Lets you manage most of your social platforms from one single dashboard. You can check and reply to messages, schedule content, monitor campaign results and more. Check it out at: hootsuite.com.

Buffer: Powerful tool that automatically posts your updates to your social media platforms at the times it thinks are the best. The posts are spaced out so your users feeds aren't clogged and your message is received. Check it out at buffer.com.

Buzzsumo: Tracks content being posted and shared on various social platforms and ranks it according to the number of shares it's getting and helps users in finding content that's trending and topics that are doing well. Check it out at buzzsumo.com.

Sprout Social: Social media management tool for

monitoring, publishing, accessing analytics and more. Check it out at sproutsocial.com.

Social Oomph: Lets you schedule updates, find quality people to follow, monitor activity on all your platforms and more. Check it out at socialoomph.com.

Social Media Marketing FAQs

What should I share besides my own content and how do I find out about hot topics?

Besides your own content, you can always share content from other pages and sites. Other sites doesn't mean your competitors sites. You can share content that is currently trending in your industry or content from sites for adjacent markets to your product. You can find out about popular topics using tools like BuzzSumo, Dig Deeper.

Should I use all of the social media platforms for my business or only use a few and master them?

You never know what's going to work well for you if you don't try so try out the popular platforms and see which ones work the best for you. Give them all a few months time and efforts before deciding whether to stick with them or not. You definitely don't have to use all of the social platforms out there and you'll rarely see a business using several platforms. Also check out what your competitors are doing: which platforms they're using and which ones seem to be going well for them.

How can I get my customers more involved and engaged?

You can give back by posting contests and giveaways on your social media. Increase engagement by asking questions. People love giving their opinion. You can ask them a question through a tweet or status update or even put up a poll. Also try putting up a few personal posts like behind the scenes posts or employee spotlights. You can have them participate in interacting more by hosting Twitter parties and Google hangouts as well.

How can I get more shares, retweets, +1's?

Try uploading an image with your post. Posts with images get a lot more attention. Also post your content at time and days when you get maximum shares. Look into your social platforms analytics to see which times your profile gets the most activity. Also keep a lookout for content that is doing well and see what did well in the past and produce more content of that type. If a large chunk of your customers reside in a particular country or region, try posting or scheduling your posts to go live according to the time zone of that area.

Should I use a tool for my social media analytics or stick to the analytics built in the platforms?

This mainly depends on your needs and how much traffic your social profiles are getting. The built in analytics are pretty good and provide a wealth of information so start off with those and if you feel you need more, you can always try out other tools.

Part 5: Content Marketing

Introduction: Content Marketing

Content marketing involves publishing information in various content formats to build trust and authority among your audience in order to acquire and obtain customers.

Everything you see online is content whichever form it may be in such as text, image, video etc. being distributed using different methods such as blogging, podcasts, webinars, infographics, slides, pdf downloads etc. All these forms and mediums of presenting your content are powerful for gaining the attention of your audience, building up your audience and slowly increasing sales by converting them from just viewers into actual customers.

Content marketing is not only important for getting your brand more out there and creating awareness and leads through readers, but also important from an optimization perspective i.e. getting fresh content out there that can be regularly indexed in search engines and ranked. Because of that it's important that every business has a blog to showcase their content on.
Content marketing is good for getting indexed and ranking in search engine, gives a voice to your business as well as your audience as they can comment on it, builds your authority and showcases you as an expert figure if done right, allows you to grow your community, build your brand and trust and more.

Steps Involved: Content Marketing

Here's a basic outline of the steps content marketing involves:

1. Choose your main topic
2. Choose your content delivery methods
3. Come up with content topics
4. Create a content marketing plan and schedule
5. Create content
6. Deliver content
7. Analyze results, improve and repeat

Explaining the above in more detail:

Choose your main topic:

This should be quite easy. Your main topic should be one that represents your business and which industry you're in. For e.g. if you're a chiropractor, you're going to be writing about different chiropractic techniques and exercises. Of course you're going to drill that down into hundreds of different topics such as chiropractic exercises for different age groups like children, seniors, exercises for different injuries, conditions and body parts, benefits of chiropractic care etc.Drilling down your main topic into various topics for content ideas will be covered in the research and content plan creation stage. Also remember that you can always get into adjacent markets when it comes to content and step outside of your main topic by getting into relevant topics. In the case of a chiropractor, instead of always writing about chiropractic techniques, you can sometimes talk about health as a topic in general.

Choose your content delivery methods:

Most people think of writing blog articles when it comes to content. But content marketing is so much more. Everything you see online is content and it takes various forms other than just articles such as videos, image galleries, info-animations, podcasts, audio recordings etc.

Here are some ideas on different formats your content can take:

1. Blog articles
2. Whitepapers
3. Market studies, research papers
4. Videos
5. Images, Image galleries
6. Infographics
7. Info-animations
8. Podcasts
9. Webinars
10. Memes
11. Guides
12. Checklists, Cheat sheets, Lists
13. Lists
14. eBooks
15. Case studies
16. Interviews

17. Quizzes
18. Tutorials

Come up With Content Topics:

Generate a list of content topics you want to write. Based on how frequently you want to post and how long you want to make the content marketing plan for, come up with the total number of topics you need. It's a good idea to create a short term plan if this is your first content plan so you can see how it performs. Creating content ideas for a few months worth of content is good to begin with. The frequency of your posts depends on your resources and content type. If you're going to be developing a lot of content that takes time such as guides and market studies, you'll probably only end up posting a few of those a year. The other content you'll be posting more regularly can be posted a few times a week. You need to keep in mind the quality and quantity factor here. If you have an entire content marketing team helping you out, you can produce quality posts more frequently. but if it's just you, post a few times a week instead of daily so you can maintain quality. You don't need to post daily, but it's a good idea to post atleast once a week. Try not to go over a week without content.

To come up with content ideas, start off by roughly brainstorming ideas you already have. Think about what you want to write about and what you think your audience will enjoy. While choosing topics always remember that your main goal for writing the content is to show your audience that you know what you're talking about and are a thought leader in your industry. Your main aim is to gain their trust and ultimately convert them from just being a reader to becoming a customer. While deciding topic, also check out what your competitors are producing. You don't need to blindly copy them but it's a good idea to see what they're up to and put your own spin to it.

Use tools to help you get content ideas based on topics people are currently searching. This is great for coming up with hot topics that can provide a lot of traffic. Use sites like Alltop (alltop.com), Google Trends (google.com/trends) and tools like Buzzsumo (buzzsumo.com) to find trending topics. Use Q and A sites like Quora (quora.com) and Yahoo Answers (answers.yahoo.com) to find out what's on people's minds and what type of content they need information on. Google Keyword Planner (adwords.google.com/KeywordPlanner) can be used to find long tail searches people are conducting around your topic. These search queries are usually question style or can be made into that. Creating content around such search queries can help bring in traffic even though their search volumes are usually low because they're easier to rank for.

When coming up with content topic ideas, also keep in mind what type of content it's going to be. and the format. Keep a good mix of topics that are currently trending and evergreen topics that will always be searched. If you only write about topics that are hot now, they'll most probably only be searched for for a short amount of time and so you'll only get traffic for them for that time period only and after that visits to that piece of content will stop.

Create a Content Marketing Plan and Schedule:

You can create a content marketing plan using fancy tools or just create a simple one using Microsoft Excel. In a new Excel sheet, set up columns for the type of content, content format, content title, keywords to target. These are just some examples of information you can have as a part of your content plan. You can add a lot more information such as structure, aim, frequency, tone, word count etc., whatever you need to keep track of. Add your content titles based on the topics you came up with before. While doing this, put them in such a sequence that you have a good mix of formats such as guides, videos, webinars, blog articles etc., and a good mix of topics that are currently trending and evergreen ones. Give each title a date for when it is to go live as well. You can also set up a content editorial calendar (wordpress.org/plugins/editorial-calendar) to see when pieces of content are supposed to go live so you can get a better idea of all of your posts.

Create Content:

Steps to keep in mind while creating content:

1. Research
2. Plan your article
3. Write
4. Format: Add images, links, videos, sources
5. Edit

While writing your content, make sure to optimize it for your target keywords as well. Your content will end up reaching a wider audience if it ranks well so add in those keywords. Also edit your content well. Your aim is to emerge as a thought leader and gain your audience's trust. You can't do that with content full of errors. Put effort and thought into your writing and write to impress your readers, not just to rank in search engines. Most people don't get content marketing right because their content quality is horrible and they do it only for ranking purposes and write just for the sake of writing and having something to put up on their site and do it just because everyone else is. Don't do that. It's easy to stand out. Just provide value. Write content that you yourself would want to read. Also add a CTA in your content. You're writing the content to convert your readers to customers so make it easy for them to see your offer by providing a CTA. Instead of having them search around your website for the purchase page, direct them to it yourself.

Deliver Your Content:

1

You can create content along the way according to your content plan, or create pieces before hand and schedule them to go live. Either way, have your content go live according to the publishing dates in your plan at a time which will bring you the maximum readers. You can choose this plan based on the timings your readers are most active on your site (check your Google Analytics account for this). Your work doesn't end once your content goes live. After that you need to promote it. Share it across your social media platforms. Producing content without optimizing or sharing is not worth it. Like performing without an audience and putting hard work into something that will never be seen. If you've published a piece of content that's more valuable than most of your regular content like a whitepaper, market study or something similar which you think is link worthy, build links to it.

Analyse Results, Improve and Repeat:

Check your Google Analytics account to see which content pieces on your site did the best so you can produce similar content like that since it worked well. Also see what times and days you got the most readers. Check out your traffic. Has it grown? What rate is it growing at? Check out the overall feedback on your content through number of shares and comments. Check your site backlinks to see if you got any links to your content from other sites.

Helpful Content Marketing Sites and Tools

Trending Topics: Find trending topics using Alltop (alltop.com), Google trends (google.com/trends), BuzzSumo (buzzsumo.com)

Google Keyword Planner: Find long tail search queries with low ranking competitiveness levels to build your content around. Check it out at adwords.google.com/keywordplanner.

Yoast SEO: Easy to use SEO plugin to optimize the content you publish. Check it out at: wordpress.org/plugins/wordpress-seo.

Trello: Tool that is helpful for organizing content ideas. Check it out at trello.com.

Graphic Creators: Picmonkey (picmonkey.com) and Canva (canva.com) can be used to create stunning images you can use in your content.

Grammarly: One step ahead of spell check, it helps in correcting your content. Check it out at grammarly.com.

Pic Resize: Easy to use image resizer you can use to resize images according to your theme measurements. Check it out at picresize.com.

Infographic Makers: Tools you can use to make

stunning infographics without a deigner: Piktochart (piktochart.com) and Infogr.am (infogr.am).

Pixabay: Best source to find free stock images to use. Check it out at pixabay.com.

Content Marketing FAQs

Can I use my social profiles for putting up content or I have to have a blog?

Using your social platforms to publish your content will have limitations such as formatting, word count, visibility. Social media is also better suited for shorter posts so a 500 word article won't look right. You can't add CTAs or capture the reader's emails in social media posts. Your blog is a better CMS with endless possibilities.

What if my industry is very boring and I don't know what topics to come up with?

There are plenty of boring industries out there for which coming up with exciting content ideas is tough. Boring industries which are tough to write exciting content about can be stove manufacturers, hanger makers etc. Content marketing for such businesses sounds tough but you can work around that with creativity and adjacent markets. In the case of a hanger manufacturer, you can create content on closet organizing tips, wardrobe decluttering tips, trends in fashion etc. In the case of the stove manufacturers, you can publish recipes or a how-to post on a DIY stove cleaning solution. There are always content ideas, even for boring industries.

How many words should my content be?

Your content quality doesn't have any link to length. A short article can be better and more useful than a longer written content many times. Keep that in mind and don't write longer articles by putting in filler content because you think they'll be received better. But at the same time, don't publish very short 100 word articles either that are really more of just a paragraph because Google can consider that as thin content and penalize you. Try keeping your content to a minimum of 300 words. If your content ends up being very long such as over 2000 words, you can always break it up into a few parts to make it easier to read.

How frequently should I post my content?

If you're short on time and resources and don't have a full content marketing team, it's better to post less so you can maintain quality. You don't have to post daily but try not to go longer than a week without posting. Ideally try posting a few times a week.

Someone stole my content. How can I have it removed or report it?

Unfortunately this happens far too often online. You can contact the website owner and request them to remove your content. If they fail to do so, report the content to Google by submitting a DCMA complaint at google.com/webmasters/tools/dmca-notice. You can also manually check if someone has stolen any of your content using Copyscape (copyscape.com).

Further Your Learning

If you'd like to take your learning further, I have an SEO Course up on my site and more books:

Other products:

SEO Course:

SEO Course Syllabus:

My SEO Course is available at **Digiologist.com** (**course page link: https://goo.gl/C43oMO**) and I have a special coupon code only for my valuable readers!

Use the coupon code Amazon for 75% off.

Course Details:

- 4.5 Hours of video tutorials
- 52 video lessons

Course Syllabus:

Setting Everything Up:

Introduction to the Course ⏱ 01:21

Methods of Digital Marketing ⏱ 03:31

How to Choose a Domain Name ⏱ 03:30

Parts of a Website Address ⏱ 05:23

How to Choose a TLD: Top Level Domain ⏱ 03:10

Different CMS Options for Your Site: Content Management Systems ⏱ 05:39

SEO Friendly Website Design and Layout Tips ⏱ 05:10

Useful WordPress Plugins for Your Site ⏱ 03:28

SEO Basics:

Introduction to SEO ⏱ 01:21

Ranking Factors Google Considers While Crawling Your Site ⏱ 07:18

Site Metrics: DA, PA, PR ⏱ 05:30

How to Check Site Metrics ⏱ 05:21

How to Create Search Strings for Targeted Searches ⏱ 09:52

How to Create Multiple Search Modifiers for Advanced Searches ⏱ 05:58

On-Page SEO:

Introduction to On-Page SEO ⏱ 01:06

Off-Page SEO: Link Building

Competitor Backlink Analysis Tutorial ⏱ 03:23

Internal Linking Tutorial ⏱ 04:11

Roundup Posts Tutorial ⏱ 03:56

Using Expired Domains & Shut Down Businesses for Link Building ⏱ 03:29

Reclaiming Links to Social Profiles and 404s ⏱ 03:34

Conduct Reverse Image Searches: Find Sites Using Your Images Without Permission ⏱ 02:26

PR Commenting for Getting Media Mentions ✎ (Written Lesson)

Q and A Sites and Forum Link Building ✎ (Written Lesson)

Directory and Submission Site Link Building ✎ (Written Lesson)

Conducting Automated Customized Bulk Outreach for Link Requests ⏱ 03:14

Recording Links Built Properly and Getting Notified of Links Deleted/Removed ⏱ 01:01

Local SEO:

Introduction to Local SEO ⏱ 01:59

Setting up Your Google My Business Page ⏱ 00:50

Location Targeted On-Site Optimization and Getting Local Links ✎ (Written Lesson)

Formatting Your NAP for Citation Building ⏱ 03:12

Finding Sites to Build Citations On ⏱ 02:32

185

Getting Google Plus Reviews ✎ (Written Lesson)

Wrap Up ✎ (Written Lesson)

Course available at https://goo.gl/C43oMO

Use the coupon code Amazon for 75% off.

Course Feedback:

Great course for beginners to intermediates SEO's. I've completed lots of course's over there year but this course teaches SEO in a unique way and managed to demonstrate areas in SEO that other courses are scared to touch. ~ Omid Irani

I loved this course because the instructor make everything easy to follow. The lessons were well made and I would recommend this course to anyone who wants to understand SEO. Just do it! ~ Juanita Abenaa

Great course. I learned a lot about on-page, off-page, keyword research. This course covers all SEO. Totally worth my time and investment. ~ Ezekiel Sokoh

I Learned a lot of fresh ideas in these videos. Very useful. You are an amazing instructor with great insights! ~ Moin Sheikh

The instructor Shivani is very well spoken, very clear and very concise. She goes in to great detail explaining all the details. The videos are great in both content and quality, and the format of the learning slides is a very sleek clean design. I would highly recommend this course to anybody

wanting to learn some SEO. Thanks Shivani. Keep up the good work. ~ David Gunner

Very informative course! One of the best SEO courses I've seen here. I love how it takes you from the extreme basics to more intermediate material very smoothly so anyone can take this course up. Highly recommend to anyone looking to build up their SEO skills beyond just the basics. ~ Rick Sharma

This course is clear with professional explanations from "Shivani Karwal". I didn't understand SEO before but this course has really helped! ~ Salem Ameziane

Focused, organized, content rich and moves at excellent pace ! Very engaging! ~ Robert Smith

Informative and useful. Excellent delivery. Thank you! ~ Soon Kheng

Fantastic quality course. It may be small but it is very powerful. Thank you Shivani. I highly recommend this course to anybody wanting to advance in SEO. ~ Gonzague Re

Course available at Digiologist.com (course page link: https://goo.gl/C43oMO)

Use the coupon code Amazon for 75% off.

Other Books by Shivani Karwal:

149 Link Building Strategy Ideas:

Available at https://goo.gl/fRahkq

SEO Dictionary:

Available at https://goo.gl/ZnerYZ

Final Thoughts

I hope you now have a better idea of SEO and some strategies you can implement for your business. I hope this book helps you in building a stronger digital profile for your business.

If you enjoyed reading this book please consider reviewing it on Amazon.

In case of any questions or feedback, you can email me at <u>shivani@digiologist.com</u>.

Thanks for reading!

- Shivani Karwal

Made in the USA
San Bernardino, CA
20 February 2017